MORE THAN
36
DAYS

Three Ordinary Men
Face Extraordinary Circumstances

Carron Barrella

More Than 36 Days
Three Ordinary Men Face Extraordinary Circumstances
by Carron Barrella

Published by
Carron Barrella
www.MoreThan36Days.com
MoreThan36Days@comcast.net

Cover and Book Design: Nick Zelinger, www.NZGraphics.com

International Standard Book Number 13: 978-0-9835728-1-7 (soft cover)

Library of Congress Control Number: 2011908313

Printed in the United States of America

Second Edition

To my husband Tommy for lovingly being the constant victim of my "shenanigans." YRMW

To my children Joey and Serena; my sun and moon.

To my parents who didn't pause when their only daughter expressed her desire to throw grenades!

Acknowledgments

My many thanks to Don, Max, and Jim for having the courage once again to dredge up their past and all the emotions, feelings and pain that entails to relive those experiences and to share them with me. I wish you all peace.

Thank you to my dearest friends Lisa MacKenzie and Rick McCoy for their unwavering support and guidance.

I am grateful to my editor, Sue Hamilton, the lighthouse, always keeping me on course and directing me home. And to Nick Zelinger, who was so generous with his time, talent – and has an obvious fear of standing still.

I am so fortunate.

Thank you all for always pushing me forward.

Author's Note:

The three men in this book are an inspiration to me and truly a treasure to have in my life. It occurred to me that I could share them with anyone destined to pick up this book.

I had two objectives in writing this book; one to bring these men to life to those not privileged to know them in person. My friends are now your friends.

The second is to preserve their stories. Too many accounts, experiences and legends are laid to rest without the opportunity to breathe life once again passing from those solitary lips to the ears of the next cycle of life.

Isn't that the beauty of a book? To be places you have never been, meet people you have never met. To live through the power and imagination limited only by you and your mind's capabilities. A book allows an author to pilot your mind, drive you there yet still you have the freedom of your own interpretation. Your imagination is ultimately still in control. The beauty of books!

This book is dedicated to all veterans everywhere who have made the dedicated pledge to blindly serve the country they love. ALL veterans pay the ultimate sacrifice for their life-changing duty in one way or another. Their commitment to a calling greater than themselves is forever respected by a grateful nation.

And to those who have experienced war all the while praying that no future generation has to suffer the same fate only to watch mankind continue to fail to learn from the past.

Foreword

The veterans meet every two weeks at a little coffee shop. This is their comfort zone. There is security in their camaraderie. As they gather around the small, wrought iron table on the patio with the smell of coffee hovering around them they glance at the familiar lined faces collected here. It isn't long before the stories and experiences begin to flow as easily and smoothly as a good bottle of wine between friends. It was a beautiful typical spring morning, the sun penetrating the thin Denver air bringing its warming rays to shine upon these men.

I consider myself just a tag-a-long. I feel like I have been given a secret gift. I am somehow allowed into this sacred assembly without feeling like an intruder. Maybe it is because I am a former Marine also and there is an unbreakable bond between Marines, a brotherhood that lasts forever. The saying goes, "Once a Marine, always a Marine." There are no ex-Marines, only Marines. The motto of the United States Marine Corps is *Semper Fidelis* which is Latin for "Always Faithful." It is the loving greeting echoed from Marine to Marine shortened to *Semper Fi*. Becoming a Marine is a transformation that is never undone. Marines live by the Corps' values and ethics their entire lives.

Maybe it is because I am a woman. They have no male pretenses. No tough image to uphold around me. They can shed tears and just be themselves. I am also a mother and the wife of a Marine. I cover all the angles. It is most likely a combination of these traits that makes our relationship unique. Or maybe it is just because they can feel and sense the respect I have for them. Some part of them is aware of how I am ever in awe of each and every one of them. Perhaps they are just happy that someone cares to listen.

Most of them have never spoken about their war experiences until recently. However, there are still elements of their stories that will remain hidden deep within them and will never pass through their lips to another. But for now they are ready to talk and there is actually someone ready to listen. These stories need to be told. The future needs to hear the sacrifices these men made for us, for the world. They all had to fight their fears and personal demons to get to the other side. They knew and hated the battle, but did what needed to be done. They don't see themselves as heroic yet define courage. It is the kind of story that will make people believe, in the end, that doing the right thing does matter, because it is these guys who make us believe and keep trying.

I have always felt that people come into our lives for a reason, that we attract the teachers and mentors we need when we need them and are truly ready to learn. The universe, through the grace of its mysterious plan, brought three gentlemen; Don Whipple, Max Brown and Jim Blane, into my life and my heart. And, in some incredible way the relationships are reciprocal. They need to tell me exactly what I need to hear.

Learning from the past is valuable because it saves the time and the pain of learning the same lesson the hard way through mistakes and consequences. I cherish these men and the education I have received (for free) listening to their stories and their truth. It is almost like living backwards, something we all dream about, being young and vigorous with decades of possibility still ahead AND the benefit of a lifetime's wisdom to appreciate the truly important things and navigate the rocky bottom of the river of life. How ironic that the knowledge you gain from life experience, the knowing that guides your decisions, isn't understandable until you make the wrong choice the first time.

Isn't life grand? By the time you start to figure it out it's almost over. It's like putting together the pieces of a giant puzzle without knowing what the result will look like. When you have just a few pieces left it all starts to make sense, all the pain and all the joy and how they fit together to create the whole of a life. So you try to make the secret of the completed puzzle tangible and lasting by explaining it to the young who don't have the time or the patience to listen and don't recognize that your puzzle is their puzzle too. Too late they wish they had paid attention.

The never ending cycle of living and learning is never boring precisely because we don't have all the answers. Yet, I want to be smart enough to listen, as best I can, to the lessons of the past and apply this wisdom to my future. I want to glean some nugget of truth that I can hold in my heart as my inner compass.

I consider myself a sponge around these three gentlemen. Not because they are scholars or visionaries, but because they are men I admire just simply for the lives they have led. They are ordinary men who have done extraordinary things in my opinion. Now, in their opinion, they were just doing what needed to be done at the time. But because of their decisions and actions they affected not only my life, but all our lives and the world. Not a small task by any means, unless of course you ask them. But since I am writing this book and not them, I will tell you from my point of view what "heroes" they truly are.

All three of these men are considered part of "The Greatest Generation." They took the initiative to be the driving force of their own destiny, rather than sit around and wait to be drafted. Each of them had the ingenuity as young, adolescent boys to want to make a difference and they also possessed the resourcefulness to know they could. They made the conscious choice to become elite members of the finest fighting force in the world. They were United States Marines. Fate challenged their decision and delivered them directly into one of the worst battles in U.S. history; the battle for Iwo Jima Island in the Pacific that secured the end of World War II in February 1945. It is not only revered by all Marines, but by all who remember the famous "Flag Rising" photograph captured by Joe Rosenthal during World War II that lifted the morale of the United States and signaled the beginning of the end of the war. It gave this nation and the world hope, a symbol to cling to in hard times that there was indeed light at the end of the tunnel.

Although Iwo Jima is a small volcanic island in the Pacific, it was incredibly large in terms of war strategy. The island is only four and half miles long and two and half miles wide with the highest peak being Mount Suribachi on the Southern end. "Iwo" means sulfur in Japanese named for the rotten egg smell of its black, sulfur sand. Iwo Jima was a stepping stone for the allied forces to gain an airstrip closer to mainland Japan for planes to refuel. Obtaining the island would eliminate the base for the perilous Japanese "Zero" fighter planes. The planes were given the nickname because of the two large, red circles on the wings representing the country's flag and it would also remove the two hour window of warning Tokyo would receive of the allied forces advance.

The defense of the island consisted of 21,000 men under the command of Tadamichi Kuribayashi. All were prepared to die in defense of their homeland and all but the one thousand that were taken prisoner did. Each solider was instructed and expected to fight to the death and to take at least ten enemy with them. Thirteen thousand yards of meticulously built ventilated tunnels were constructed underground including well manufactured hospitals. One thousand cave entrances and pill boxes existed on Mount Suribachi alone to thoroughly protect the high ground. The seventy days of intense U.S. bombing intended to soften up the island in preparation for the Marine landing appeared to merely dent the resistance. The Marines were forced to struggle and violently fight for every yard of earth slowly gained.

On the fourth day Lieutenant Schrier, Platoon Sergeant Ernest Thomas, Sergeant Hansen, Corporal Lindberg, Private First Class Louis Charlo and Private First Class Raymond Jacobs hoisted the American flag atop Mount Suribachi to the cheers and roar of the men below.

Watching from a ship off the island, Secretary of the Navy James Forrestal exclaimed that the raising of the flag secures the Marine Corps for the next 500 years and he wanted the flag as a souvenir. Colonel Chandler Johnson upset by this request ordered another patrol to remove that flag and replace it with a larger one. This larger flag had been recovered from a sinking ship at Pearl Harbor and was placed on Mount Suribachi by Ira Hayes, Franklin Sousley, John Bradley (Navy Corpsman), Harlon Block, Mike Strank and Rene Gagnon. They were unaware at the time that this second flag raising was captured by photographer Joe Rosenthal, earned him a Pulitzer Prize, was successfully used for the war bond drive and forever etched into history.

Although the high ground was achieved, the fierce battles raged on until March 26 when the U.S. victory on Iwo Jima was declared.

Serving as a U.S. Marine during this legendary time is just a small glimpse of who Don, Max and Jim are, however, as with all life experience it contributed to shaping them into amazing men.

Even though they shared the same experience during the same time on that small island in the middle of the faraway ocean it wasn't until the late 1990s that they actually met each other.

They had fulfilled their obligations to the country and the world and had all returned safely home. Their focus turned to creating their lives, starting families and simply living the American dream they had a part in protecting. They each eventually chose to settle down in colorful Denver, Colorado.

It was as if a great plan had been slowly set in motion preparing them, swirling around them in the universe, timing and arranging their meeting for when each man was ready to face his past. Until this point their lives had been running parallel and finally converged as the three of them instantly connected. The similarities melted sixty years away as quickly as a January snowflake when it touches your tongue.

A Marine can immediately sense the presence of another Marine. The familiar stance of confidence and disposition can be felt as they gravitate to one another across a crowded room, as well as across generations. The Marine Corps still makes Marines the same way it always has for over 200 years. The friendship is always instantaneous, but my meeting of these three men qualified as something more. It was some sort of force that drew us together not just as Marines but seemingly for a purpose.

I have a suspicion as to who may have assisted in conjuring up this alliance.

Staff Sergeant Ed Cooper settled in North Denver upon his release from the Marine Corps in 1952. As was common he did not feel comfortable in civilian life and missed the comfort and camaraderie of his fellow *Devil Dogs*. This nickname, translated from *Teufel Hunden*, was what the Germans referred to the U.S. Marines as during the Battle of Belleau Wood during World War I, and the moniker stuck.

So Ed Cooper organized a monthly gathering of Denver area Marines. There would be no dues, no rank and no roles within the *club*. It was intended as just a time to get together, relax, eat and share experiences. Upon his death in 1999, the Marines continued to meet and called themselves Cooper's Troopers in his honor.

Cooper's Troopers has grown to well over 100 attendees strong. As a member of the Women Marines Association (WMA) I attended Cooper's Troopers where my life was thankfully changed forever. Cooper's Troopers is an exceptional group. Marines and Navy from every era are represented there and unite under the American Legion roof into one solid mass of mutual respect and equality. Don, Max and Jim personify the aura that drew me in. Learning from these three men is a gift and being their friend is an honor.

I also look forward to our regular Wednesday coffee breaks to keep perspective on what really matters. At more than twice my age, over eighty years old, they recharge *MY* battery.

After we exchange the daily pleasantries and remark on what a beautiful day has been bestowed upon us that I begin to prod them all to hear their entire stories and it is Don who begins first.

To Denise... Thanks for reading our stories of back in the day when we were just boys on Iwo Jima Feb 19 1945

Iwo Jima — Feb 19, 1945
Nagasaki Sept 1945 to April 1946

Don Whipp

5th Marine Div
28th Combat Team
13th Artillery Regt.

See Bible N.T. I Cor 15:58

God Bless you Real good

DON WHIPPLE

A man of courage is also full of faith.
— Marcus Tullius Cicero

Don Whipple has a large, contagious smile that is never out of place and often you find yourself smiling too in an unconscious reaction to the warmth that illuminates from his soul – from the very core of who he is and how he lives his life. Don would tell you that the warmth is a projection of Jesus in his heart. Don found Jesus while in the Marines and it changed the course of his life to one of service and ministry.

I agree with Don, to a point, that the warmth is a gift from God. It is a light that burns from within him and spreads to everyone he meets. He is like a child walking through a crowd with a lit sparkler on the Fourth of July. The sparks fly indiscriminately and give a little shock to everyone they contact and inexplicably the shock is welcomed.

Don has a measure of peace that is uncommon and it has nestled in and made a home in his heart. It is the kind of peace that every man yearns for. Peace that lets you sleep like a baby at night and wake up the next morning excited and grateful for a new day. The kind of serenity that lets you fully accept the things in life that you cannot change. It is this sense of tranquility and warmth that emits from Don that draws you in like a moth to a flame and you willingly succumb to it. I believe Don was born with this trait when he entered the world on August 31, 1925. I also believe that he was significantly influenced by his Mother, the dedication of his life to Jesus and his experiences as a Marine in the war.

Don was raised on a farm in the small town of Beeler, Kansas, just north of Dodge City. He was one of thirteen children with eight brothers and four sisters. He laughs recalling that he thought everyone slept four to a bed until he joined the Marines. Don attended a country day school in which the student population consisted mainly of his very own siblings. He later attended Beeler High School which boasted a total of thirty-five students. Don claims to have been a pretty good athlete, but a poor student. He bragged he never once took a book home to study. He played basketball as there were not enough boys for a football team and graduated, from Beeler, in 1943.

His childhood was typical for a boy growing up in the American heartland in the 1930s. He helped his brothers milk the cows and do other chores before school every morning while their mother prepared hot biscuits, gravy and sausage for her collection of children. For extra money to help the family get by, the boys broke wild horses on the weekends and trapped animals to sell the hides. The Whipple homestead sat on a hill in the middle of a farm of several thousand acres and afforded the family a stunning view of the three surrounding towns, yet they had no electricity or indoor plumbing. The boys would fetch and haul water to the house daily. They joked that one path was for the hot water and the other path for the cold. They took baths once a week and teased about who would be unlucky enough to end up with the last cold, dirty bath.

Don also remembers the hard edge of Midwestern farming life. There were vicious dust storms that would turn day into night. Their mother would give them wet rags to place over their faces at night so they could sleep without choking. The relentless storms left a covering of dust and grit on absolutely everything. Another summer memory involved rattlesnakes. One year the boys counted 160 snakes in one field. Don explains you can always tell a rattlesnake by the sound. A locust can make a very similar sound, but once a person has had their first encounter with a rattler you will forever know the difference. All things considered, life was simple and good for the Whipple family.

Don's grandparents lived thirty minutes away in Bazine, Kansas, where every year the town celebrates the Christmas season with a hearty, much anticipated, community breakfast. Don's family always wanted to be the first in line for the feast, but Don's grandfather would not allow them to leave before midnight. Don recalls his father standing by the car staring intently at his pocket watch and then racing them off at the stroke of midnight. The meal was incredible. His grandfather would butcher two hogs for a mountain of sausages and the biscuits and gravy seemed to flow on forever. For the Whipple family it was always the highlight of the year.

One afternoon, following the yearly celebration, Don's family was gathered around his uncle's new car, their bellies full and their spirits light. Don's uncle worked for the railroad so he had a little more money than the farming families at the time and his new car sported an actual radio. As they turned the dial the squeak and static was replaced by the slightly clearer sound of a broadcast station. As they admired the novelty they heard the sobering news of the Japanese attack on Pearl Harbor.

In school the next day the children and teachers listened intently to the radio as President Roosevelt addressed the nation with the, now famous, "Pearl Harbor speech" and the declaration of war. Don remembers feeling scared about the changes the news was bringing, but also angry at the affront to America and the loss of life. He felt anxious and compelled to get involved and do his part. Don had read the book *They Were Expendable* by William L. White recounting the PT boats conflict in the Philippines, which was later made into a movie starring John Wayne. However, Don admits it was an article in *Life* magazine that made him yearn to be a Marine. The article included pictures of Marines storming the beach at Guadalcanal. They were the first images of war Don had ever seen and they left an indelible impression.

After graduation in June 1943, Don took a train to Denver, Colorado, the location of the nearest recruiting station, with the intention of enlisting in the United States Marine Corps. He soon found himself on a train back to Kansas, however, as he was not yet eighteen and needed written permission from his parents. Although Don was only in Denver for a short time he was fascinated by the big city, starting with the fact that it had traffic lights, something he had never seen before. Once back in Kansas he worked the fields waiting for the call of duty to come. He was finally sworn in and boarded a train bound for Pueblo, Colorado on August 23, 1943, eight days shy of his eighteenth birthday.

Don couldn't help but feel he was on the adventure of a lifetime and truly it was the start of an amazing life journey. As the train headed for California, Don was very excited about seeing the ocean for the first time. He sat glued to the window, waiting to catch a glimpse of sand and surf only to be disappointed when they arrived in Los Angeles at night and he couldn't see anything. Unbeknownst to the young, eager, farm boy from Kansas he would soon be spending more time in and on the ocean than he ever anticipated.

Shortly after arriving in Los Angeles, Don encountered several Marines relaxing on the grass, their rifles resting against a tree. They yelled over to Don, "You'll be sorry." Don heard the phrase repeated many times over the coming weeks, but he never really grasped the meaning at the time. He went from Los Angeles to the recruit depot in San Diego where he began basic training, otherwise known as "boot camp." The base was covered with camouflage netting and Don remembers it seemed like a big tunnel. He still hoped to catch a good look at the ocean. Don was five foot eight and half inches tall which was an average height for a man in the 1940s and he claims to have blended in well during boot camp. Every Marine will tell you it is much better to blend in than to stand out during those first brutal sixteen weeks. Don chuckles now that, in his eighth decade, he stands only five foot seven inches. He made it through boot camp and finally earned the title of Marine.

After boot camp Don attended telephone school in Pine Valley, California, a town very close to the Arizona border. During that time Don enjoyed thirty not-so-glorious days of mess duty serving chow to the other Marines. Pine Valley was a beautiful wooded area perfect for learning to string wire through bushes and tree tops. From there Don was sent to Area 17 of Camp Pendleton where the Corps was forming the 5th Marine Division. They trained on 75 mm howitzers and Don became a forward observer. He learned the tools and tricks of the trade; splicing wire, cranking the telephone equipment and checking the lines functionality. Don laughs as he remembers the artillery starting several fires as live rounds hit the dry grass and the Marines would spend the next few days on the fire line fighting the fires instead of training.

The Marines of the 5th Division practiced beach landings over and over and over. They trained for days on Coronado beach. Here Don was, a boy from Kansas, the only state in the union without a natural lake, spending every day at the ocean. One day, storming the beach as usual, the Marines found themselves face-to-face with a startled group of picnickers. Don laughs as he wonders aloud what must have gone through their minds as the invasion force came upon them. Although there were some lighthearted moments, Don feels that the unforgiving beach landing practice was what truly prepared them for the mission to come and it was this training, along with the other brave men of the 5th Division that he credits for his survival. Before their training was completed, President Roosevelt came to the beach to observe. Don marveled at the long line of black cars and limousines and knew that they must be training for something very important.

It was time for the Marines to continue their preparations in another location and they shipped out with no idea where they were going. As the saying goes, "Loose lips sink ships." Although there was no official information, rumors, or "scuttlebutt" as it is known in the military, abounded. Don spent the days taking in the unfamiliar environment of the open sea, marveling at how it changed from day to day, hour to hour. Sometimes it was flat as a pane of glass without a ripple and other times it was violent and raging with a myriad of states in between the two extremes.

The ship docked in Hilo, Hawaii, and after disembarking the Marines finished their trek to the make-shift base in simple box cars normally used for transporting sugar cane. The Hawaiians greeted them warmly and gave them freshly harvested pineapple and sugar cane. Don was a little shocked to see a cattle ranch on the island as he had just assumed the Hawaiian island consisted of only exotic fruit and hula girls. These Hawaiian cowboys intrigued the farm boy from Kansas. The Marines lived in tents referred to as Camp Tarawa and continued their training.

It was during this time that Don met a fellow Marine named Bill Johnson and this meeting was the spark that lit the fire of purpose and dedication that would come to define the rest of Don's life. Bill Johnson invited him to a church service. Curious, Don accepted the invitation and was so inspired by the peace and joy he found that he knew it was what he wanted for his life.

The Marines training continued day in and day out. They had a map to guide their training and one day Don noticed a newspaper article that detailed the bombing campaign currently being waged on the South Pacific island of Iwo Jima. He thought the photo of the island looked similar to their training map. Several more months passed with no variation in the routine and finally, just before Christmas, the Marines began loading up ships for a planned January 1 departure. Don remembers an exhaustive inspection was held that included all of their gear and confirmed everything was accounted for; weapons, tools, etc.

The 5th Division took in new members and was clearly being overstaffed. A young Marine, trained in communications, named Bob Heplerly, was added to their unit. Don felt compassion for Bob because he joined the already cohesive unit late without the opportunity to train and become familiar with the other men. Don went out of his way to welcome and befriend Bob. Don learned that Bob had a brother who was a Navy pilot and they both took leave to visit him. Don quietly recalls Bob saying goodbye to his brother explaining he just felt he wasn't going to make it.

When it was time to depart, the Marines loaded on liberty ships. The entire harbor was lined with ships as far as the eye could see. It was an impressive sight. Don recalled all of the practice they had unloading from ships; climbing down the rope ladders and cargo nets then dropping eight feet to land in a boat bucking and turning with the movement of the choppy water. It was an experience not soon forgotten. Don was proud of the division's hard work and training. Surely they must have practiced beach landings a thousand times. They were as ready as they could be for whatever awaited them as the ships headed to meet the enemy in, as yet unknown, distant lands.

Don recalled the last time he was home on leave. It had been only Don and his father at the train station in Dodge City that day as he prepared to return to duty. Don boarded the train and sat down in his seat. His father followed him on the train and stood over him trying to say his goodbyes. Uncharacteristically, his father leaned down and kissed him on the lips. He hadn't done that since Don was a little boy. Don thought of himself as a tough Marine and here his father was kissing him as if he were a child. Maybe Don's father had the intuition to know that this would be their last goodbye or maybe it was just a response to what goes through a father's mind as he sends his child off to war. Sixty years later the thought of his last moments with his Father still bring tears to Don's eyes.

Don's father Jacob was killed while Don was on his way to Iwo Jima. Rubber tires were rationed at the time and one day while driving home, one of Jacob's tires, worn thin with overuse, went flat. He was at the side of the road changing the tire when he was struck by a drunk driver and dragged beneath his car. The driver was too drunk to help Jacob so it was Don's mother Bernice and his younger brother Rex that extracted Jacob from the wreck and took him to the hospital. Jacob died of his injuries within a few hours. The entire Whipple family took the loss of the head of the family hard, but none were quite as devastated as Rex. Six weeks later Don received a letter from his aunt expressing sympathy for his loss. Confused, Don sent a telegram home asking what had happened and it was then he learned of his father's death. Months later Don finally received his mother's original, tear-stained letter that had been delayed in the military mail.

The rally point in the harbor of Saipan was an incomprehensible mass of ships, aircraft carriers and destroyers. Don remembers watching from the deck as a single submarine made its way through the maze out to open water. Even though the island had been bombed without reprieve for the past seventy days to loosen it up, the bombing campaign proved almost futile. The entire island was "honeycombed" by the Japanese. It was an underground fortress, an elaborate web of intricate mazes, tunnels and caves. The Japanese were not merely on the island, they were in it. Never the less, the stage was set, it was time.

The Marines were out of their racks by 3:00 a.m. on that fateful morning of February 19, 1945. The order of the day was to be in cleaned, pressed dungarees with their faces clean shaven. They were served a full meal; turkey, stuffing, sweet potatoes and pumpkin pie. It felt like the last meal of condemned men.

Don felt anxious but ready as the constant bellow of the bombing pounded in his ears and radiated through to his skull. The Marines training was now second nature and they felt ready to do their duty. It was not quite dawn when they finished breakfast and the men could just make out the silhouette of the island illuminated by the flashes of the continual shelling and bombardment. Don felt surely there was no more awesome sight than the gun turrets of a battleship. The barrage was unrelenting and it rose in intensity until it was a steady rhythm, as 5,000 tons of explosives were unleashed in a deafening roar on the island courtesy of the battleships "North Carolina," "Washington," "New York," "Arkansas" and "Nevada." With scores of destroyers, mine sweepers and submarines participating in the mission; it was the largest armada invasion up to that time in history.

At 6:00 a.m. the Marines were over the side of the ship and into the landing crafts. Each carried a pack, rifle, ammo, bed roll, gas mask, and any other equipment specific to their duty. The sea was rough as they circled around until every man was loaded. His stomach clenching, Don thought how ironic it was that he had never been sea sick until that moment as he lost every bit of the last fine meal. As he watched the dive bombers overhead the reality of the situation started to sink in, this was not a drill. All of the training and practice had been in preparation for this horrible day.

It was five minutes to H-Hour and Don watched, mesmerized, as a fighter plane was hit by anti-aircraft fire. It sputtered and spiraled downward, disappearing into the sea. Don learned later that the pilot's wife had given him a baby girl eight days earlier. Such is war. A landing craft near them suffered a direct hit and Don could feel the heat of the fireball on his face. He stared in horror as the explosion sent bodies flying through the air in every direction. The "You'll be sorry" warning from those Marines back in San Diego floated through his mind.

At 9:00 a.m. everything stopped. It was deadly calm and the sudden absence of sound was unnerving. Don was assigned to the second wave instructed to land on what was referred to in the mission plan as "Green" beach closest to Mount Suribachi. As the landing craft made its way to shore the men were forced to their knees for stability as the craft rocked violently in the wake of those ahead of them.

A man that Don would come to revere, Captain Austin, said to Don, "Isn't this a horrible way to spend your birthday?"

Don stared at him and asked his age.

His Captain responded, "Twenty-four".

Don remembers that, at the time, it seemed that Austin was an old man as the average age of the entire 5th Marine Division was nineteen. Don chuckles that WWII was won by nothing but a bunch of teenagers.

Nearing the shore, the landing craft maneuvered in as quickly as possible in an attempt to unload the men on dry sand. Wham! The ramp door was down and the Marines stormed out. Don's mouth was so dry he couldn't utter a sound. He could barely swallow. In the shallow water, the men laden with gear trudged toward the dry land, a sense of doom hanging over them like the lingering thick clouds of smoke in the air.

Luckily, the enemy resistance to the first waves was light and sporadic. The Japanese were waiting for the Marines to come ashore before commencing the attack in earnest. The sand was black, volcanic ash and the Marines sunk up to their ankles as they assaulted. The telephone equipment was loaded into a cart but it was soon immovable, past its axles in the sand. The men tied ropes to the corners and tried to drag the heavy cart while more men pushed from behind.

So focused on his task, Don was not aware of the mortar until he was knocked flat. Dazed, Don tried to get to his feet. Captain Austin was by his side and helped him stand. As the captain explained to Don that he had been hit, Don noticed the blood flowing out of his pant leg, beginning to cover his boot and puddle in the sand. Captain Austin helped him slip into a shell crater as it was the nearest site that afforded any cover from the devastation that rained down on them. Captain Austin assisted another wounded Marine into the crater as well and left them to summon a corpsman.

The men were eventually taken to an aid station that was already overwhelmed with wounded and dying men. Don suffered a concussion from the mortar blast and cannot recollect any other details. The first day of hell was coming to a close and it was growing dark as Don was taken to the beach to wait for transport to a hospital ship. He was propped up against a wall next to another Marine on a stretcher. The Marine had no skin on his face or anywhere else on the front of his body. Don could clearly see his heart beating, struggling to maintain life even as the blood and fluids of his body seeped from his massive wounds. Don couldn't understand how the man could still be alive and so he offered the only aid he could think of – he leaned his head back against the wall and prayed.

The wounded were loaded on a boat and made their way to the closest makeshift hospital ship. There were not enough hospital ships for the mission so troop ships were converted. As they approached, the air raid sirens sounded and smoke was released to protect the ships. The first ship informed them that they were full and could not take in any more men. Maneuvering through the cold, choppy water in the smoke they approached several more ships, each gave the same response. Desperation grew as precious time slipped away and it seemed help for the wounded men would remain just out of reach. Finally, the Navy lieutenant who operated their boat stood his ground and shouted they weren't moving until the ship agreed to take them in. He demanded that the wounded needed help and they would get it now!

Don recounts this event with silent tears sliding down his cheeks as he is ever grateful to this brave, compassionate Navy lieutenant for standing defiant until the ship took them in.

Once aboard, the crew on the ship tended to the men's wounds. The shrapnel in Don's leg was so close to bone they decided not to remove it. There was a Marine in the bunk under Don's that looked like he was barely sixteen-years-old. His face was drained of the normal color that usually accompanies life and his pallor was ashen. Both of his legs were gone. The air raid sirens sounded again and Don was afraid the ship would be hit. He wasn't so much afraid for his own safety, but rather for the young Marine. Don knew he couldn't take much more. There was a terrible, piercing noise as the ship's radar tower was hit. Again, Don did the only thing he could for the boy, he prayed. Thankfully, the ship avoided any other hits that night.

The next morning it was announced that the ship's crew was preparing to conduct a burial at sea and Don went to pay his respects to the fallen. He was gripped with an overwhelming lonely, empty feeling. Don thought of the men, half a world away from everything they knew and loved and the people who loved them. It just wasn't fair. The heartbreaking sadness he felt as the bodies disappeared beneath the waves would stay with him for the rest of his life.

From the deck, Don could see the island. Even from a distance it looked like all hell was breaking loose. Tracer bullets could be seen in steady streams and the constant shelling, if anything was increasing. Don sadly wondered to himself if anyone at all would leave the island alive.

It was announced that the ship would head to Guam the next day. Don wanted to return to his Marines and his duty. He couldn't comprehend leaving alone without them. He saw a mechanic repairing a landing craft and asked if he was planning to go back ashore. The mechanic replied that he was planning to return to Iwo the next morning and Don was welcome to hitch a ride if he could find a uniform to wear. In the center of the ship's deck was the "dead man's pile." It was a mountain of uniforms formerly worn by fallen men. Don scrounged around and found one that would suffice. He scratched off the dead Marine's name and put it on. The next morning Don found himself on the "Green" beach for a second time. He noticed a truck loading up with ammunition and recognized the driver. Don caught a ride and was able to find, and rejoin, his unit.

Back with his unit, Don busied himself directing fire into the caves on the slopes of Mt. Suribachi, ignoring the pandemonium all around him. There was chatter on the phone lines about a flag raising and Don was able to witness both of them, the first spontaneous raising of the American flag, and the second famous flag raising captured by photographer Joe Rosenthal. The ships blew their horns and the men cheered. For a moment the island seemed alive again and the presence of death lifted for a few wonderful moments as the Marines captured the high ground. Sadly, however, the worst was yet to come.

Don's unit trekked farther up the mountain passing other Marines as they headed down for some relief, Don believes they were the men of the 27th Marines. Most staggered and Don described them as walking zombies. They were in complete shell shock. Their eyes empty of any emotion, stared blank and vacant, their faces expressionless. Some, less conscious part of their minds had taken over to protect them because what they had experienced was too much to bear.

Don wondered how war could ever seem like an answer. Why couldn't mankind just figure out a way to move forward without devastation and destruction? The experience of war is impossible to put into words or even convey with pictures. People can't really understand it unless they have lived it, and if they have lived it they are forever changed by it.

The battle for Iwo Jima raged on and on. It was never truly dark on the island. At night, the constant flares sent up by the battleships and destroyers, used to thwart surprise attacks, gave the illusion of perpetual dawn.

The *Star Spangled Banner* is a very meaningful song for Don. Aside from the messages of hope and patriotism it offers all Americans, two phrases seem uniquely significant to him. The phrase "by dawn's early light" brings to mind images of the island where it seemed the sun never set. The phrase "the flag was still there" reminds Don of the countless times he glanced up at Mount Suribachi to make sure the flag was still there. The air of Iwo Jima hung heavy with the stench of death, diesel fuel and sulfur and none of the men would ever be able to fully purge the smell from their consciousness.

Don recalls the lack of normalcy on the island. For example, the Marines carried their food called C-Rations. The meal allotment was individually canned and pre-cooked issued to U.S. Forces from 1938-1958. The A-Ration was fresh food. Chow prepared in a field kitchen or mess hall was considered a B-Ration. Rations were eventually replaced with the MCI – Meal Combat Individual and then in 1980 with the modern day MRE – Meal Ready to Eat. Mealtime, something a Marine normally looked forward to, held no pleasure. It just became a necessity, fuel, to allow an exhausted, aching body to continue for a few more hours. The normal, social aspect of eating together did not exist on Iwo. It seemed all the simple facets of life, the feeling of being human had disappeared. Don doesn't even remember relieving himself. The Marines were machines.

One night a phone line was cut and the problem area needed to be found and repaired. Captain Austin called the men together to brief them and discuss options just as a "spider trap" door opened. A Japanese soldier popped up and fired a single round that went right through Bob Heplerly's head. Captain Austin cradled Bob in his arms and comforted him until the quivering of his body mercifully ended. Captain Austin gently carried Bob's lifeless body over to the Corpsmen and told them to give him a proper burial. He explained that he was going to talk to Bob's parents personally and wanted to be able to ensure them that their son was laid to rest with respect. In the presence of that caring gesture it was as if time stood still for one tender moment. The juxtaposition of such gentle compassion amid the chaos and devastation seemed bizarre. Such a caring, loving gesture at this time, in this place, was incredibly hopeful. It reminded Don of a tiny, beautiful flower breaking through a heavy blanket of new snow to stand tall and proud against the winter.

The battle roared on for weeks. On the thirty-fifth night the Marines were promised a shower and a hot meal on the ship. Don and a few other men sat on an artillery gun waiting to leave when the photographer, Joe Rosenthal, took their picture. Don would always wonder what became of it. But as the Marines waited they watched a group a mechanics head out to repair some B29's. Suddenly, a Japanese pilot orchestrated a "banzai" attack on the planes and the mechanics were all killed. Others suffered bayonet stabs right through the thin walls of their tents as they slept. Death on the island had become the norm, but Don wondered at the paradox of surviving thirty-five days of hell only to be killed so near the end of the campaign.

After 864 hours of fighting the Japanese were defeated and the battle for the island of Iwo Jima was finally over. More Medals of Honor were awarded to U.S. Marines on Iwo than in any other battle in history. One in three men who fought in the battle were either killed or wounded resulting in a total of 25,851 casualties. Of those, 6,825 men paid the ultimate price for freedom on the island. More than 20,000 Japanese soldiers also perished. Before Don left he visited some graves and had the sad, empty feeling of leaving his friends behind. He never wanted to see the hellish island again.

He recalls that none of the Marines even looked back as they left. It was the ugliest place on earth. Don felt happy and sad at the same time. He was so overwhelmed he leaned against the wall, slowly slid down it and sat and cried. There was simply no other way to release the emotion – the crushing burden of the last thirty-six days.

Don saw some incredible acts of heroism while on the island and felt Admiral Nimitz, Commander in Chief of the Pacific Fleet, said it best, "Uncommon valor was a common virtue." But Don felt that the greatest heroes of the battle for Iwo Jima and of military life in general were the mothers, wives, fathers and other loved ones back home who had no control over the situation and could do nothing more than pray and wait at the mercy for news, whatever it might be.

Don recalled an interesting interview with General Holland M. Smith, nicknamed "Howlin' Mad" because of his toughness and hard-driving ethics even by Marine Corps standards. Smith commanded the Fleet Marine Force in the Pacific. He was asked by a journalist if he ever felt the Marines would get pushed off the island to which he replied, no, it had never entered his mind. Marines had never before or ever will be pushed off an island. Although he admitted lying awake many nights worried that there would be enough men left for a dedication at the cemetery.

Finally back aboard the ship, Don remembers docking one more time to allow Ira Hayes, one of the Marines in the flag raising photo, off the boat so he could be flown back to the U.S. for a war bond promotion tour. Don had no idea; none of the Marines did, of the notoriety the battle received back in the states. Their orders were to wait on reserve just off the coast to assist in the fight to seize the island of Okinawa. Don thanked God that the orders were changed because of the high number of casualties and they were allowed to return to Hawaii instead. When they docked in Hawaii, the men were stunned to hear newspaper boys shouting that President Franklin D. Roosevelt was dead.

After a short respite and more training in Hawaii, the men shipped out, once again, this time as part of "Operation Olympia" with orders to invade the Japanese mainland. Their ship was in total blackout when they received the news of the dropping of the atomic bombs and the subsequent Japanese surrender. Suddenly, the ships sprang to life as all of the lights came on. As the men celebrated the end of the war, the illuminated ships lit up the ocean like a Christmas tree.

Sixty years later, Don struggles against the lump in his throat to accurately express the sense of gratitude and relief that came over him as he realized the fighting was truly over.

The ship continued on and eventually docked in Sasebo, Japan. American POW's were being released from captivity. The once young and strong men were a gut-wrenching sight. They were walking skeletons – just a thin layer of skin stretched over bone. Don's unit began patrolling the hills and caves of Sasebo. Their mission was to find any war equipment they could; telescopes, radios, cameras, etc. They collected their finds during the day and piled them in the streets to be destroyed at night.

It wasn't long before the men noticed Japanese children watching them with curiosity so the Marines would give them candy. As children are known to do, they worked their magic breaking down barriers between strangers with their openness and innocence. Soon the Marines were sitting with entire families, laughing and teaching each other American and Japanese folk songs. Looking at the group it was hard to imagine that a few weeks earlier they were enemies engaged in brutal fighting against one another.

As Don enjoyed the sense of community he considered himself to be one of the lucky ones. After he was wounded, he was allowed to return to duty on the island and because of that he was able to achieve a measure of peace with the situation, as he watched events unfold and eventually conclude. He completely understood how men who were wounded and not allowed back could harbor intense feelings of resentment.

The 5th Marine Division was disbanded and the men were sent to join the 2nd Marine Division in Nagasaki where they stood guard duty around the atomic bomb crater near the train railhead. The Japanese refugees were a study in human suffering. The experience that still weighs on Don's heart was transporting garbage to the dump site. Orphaned children lived at the dump and would climb on the trucks, as soon as they entered, practically attacking the men to get a few scraps of food. The Marines were forced to use the butts of their rifles to gently push the naked, filthy children, driven mad with hunger, away from the vehicles.

Don also had one of his scariest moments while on guard duty. As he patrolled the perimeter one morning just before dawn, he heard rustling in the bushes that lined a nearby ditch. Worried it was an ambush Don called out the challenge phrase. When he heard no response he was sure the noise was a diversion designed to allow another enemy to come up behind him and slit his throat. Though afraid, Don didn't fire. He took a few deep breaths and remembered the rattlesnakes in the field back home. He felt that if someone was there he would just know it in the same way he never had to ask twice if he heard a rattler.

The men were stationed in Nagasaki for nine months. The area had been wiped flat clean by the bomb blast. Absolutely nothing of the former thriving city remained other than some twisted steel that could be seen in the distance. The men were never warned about possible dangers of radiation so no one worried about their extended exposure to ground zero. Don jokes now that if he is glowing it is simply his high intelligence and has nothing to do with radiation.

In March 1946, Don Whipple's duty to the Marine Corps was complete and he was, at long last, headed home. The entire trip would take twenty-one days. In San Diego the returning troops were welcomed home as heroes. Planes flew in formation overhead, bands played patriotic songs, and fire boats sprayed water into the air. The fanfare was nice, but paled in comparison to the gift Don received from the Navy Mothers Organization – milk and cookies. Don was ecstatic to drink beautiful, creamy, rich, cold milk once again. It had been a very long time. It was a huge reminder that the simple things in life are beautiful.

As Don boarded the train that would take him back to Dodge City, Kansas, he felt he had lived a lifetime since leaving home. Don's mother, siblings and soon-to-be wife, Joan, were all at the station, excited to welcome him back. Don knew his father would not be at the station, yet it struck him as hard as a physical blow to the chest when his father's face was absent from the smiling crowd. It is when a family is together that the loss of a loved one is felt most keenly – the ache of remembering what once was and can never be again is forever a raw wound no matter how much love there is for the people that remain.

Don's thoughts returned to his father's kiss as he left, it seemed to make sense now. He wished he could have attended his father's funeral. He needed a sense of closure that wouldn't ever seem to come. The sense of loss slowly faded into the background as his family fussed and treated him like a king. His mother cooked every one of his favorite meals.

Don and his fiancée, Joan, had known each other since they were three-years-old. It seemed they had always been together. They married in November 1946 when Don attended radio school in Kansas City and Joan worked for the telephone company. They suffered three miscarried pregnancies, possibly because of Don's exposure to radiation in Nagasaki, before being blessed with a baby girl, Debbie, in October 1954. Debbie is currently a nurse in Denver, Colorado.

After radio school, Don found work at a radio station. The son of the station's owner had been a Marine and was killed in the war. The man took a special interest in Don and encouraged him to continue his education. He made the commitment that once Don completed his education he would hire him to manage his radio stations. Don took his advice and moved to Colorado to attend Denver University. To make ends meet, Don drove buses and streetcars down Broadway and Colfax, the main arteries of the city at the time. Eventually, Don transferred from DU to what is now Colorado Christian College where he finished his education.

Over the years the shrapnel in Don's leg started to shift away from the bone. As it worked its way closer to the surface of his skin, it grew more painful. Eventually Don had it removed.

Don's ultimate passion, and the mission of his life, was to share the word of the Bible and let everyone know that God loves them. His dedication to spread the word led him, and his family, all over the globe. They lived in Singapore from 1960 to 1965. Don mentored young pastors in Costa Rica. He also found time to work with numerous high school youth organizations. Don's life has been defined by service. When he completed his service to his country, he committed himself to a life of service spreading God's word and his message of love to the world.

After nearly sixty years of marriage it was an immeasurable loss to Don when he lost Joan in 2003. He held her and prayed with her as she passed. He was reminded of Captain Austin cradling Bob Heplerly in his arms so many years ago. Don's life was touched by many brave people but he considers his personal heroes to be his mother and Captain Austin. He loves to tell stories of courageous people. Some touched his life personally, while others he grew to love and admire through books. There was a man named Jim Elliot who was killed by South American rebels while he was on God's mission there. There was also Corrie Ten Boom, the amazing woman who was held as a political prisoner in Nazi concentration camps for hiding Jews. Don feels her life embodied the true meaning of the word forgiveness.

Don gives all credit to God for any ability he has in influencing the lives of others and assisting them in finding Jesus. He considers courage to be the ability to act even in fear. He encourages future generations to establish a relationship with Jesus at their earliest opportunity, and that relationship will guide every other aspect of their lives. Don feels the most influential event in his life was meeting Bill Johnson, the Marine who invited him to church and introduced him to Jesus.

Don's story begins and ends with Bill Johnson. As Don sighs and slowly lowers his head I realize, as I look at him, that he is one of the most beautiful people I have ever seen. He glows. Unexpectedly, the word *glorious* comes into my mind. Don Whipple is, and will always be, my hero. He embodies all of the qualities I admire; courage, integrity, passion, commitment and peace. He dedicates himself fully to his tasks and simply lives his life with an almost inconceivable amount of faith.

The Whipple family

The Whipple farmhouse

Don's brothers
Paul (left), Rex (middle),
Tom (right)

A Young Don

Young Marine, Don Whipple

Don, Mom, Grandpa Gilmore
You can see where he got his dazzling smile!

Troop transport ship

On deck

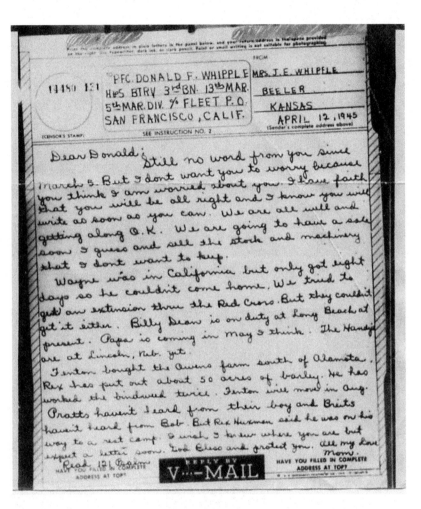

V-Mail letter from Mom

Capt. Austin, Dr. Zdanis (1945)

Capt. Austin, Fred Serral (1990s)

Don and wife Jo with their daughter Debbie (1960s)

Don and wife Jo

MAX BROWN

I have a simple philosophy: Fill what's empty.
Empty what's full. Scratch where it itches.
— Alice Roosevelt Longworth

Max Brown has a soft-spoken, understated charm that is so alluring and inviting it is truly impossible to resist, though no one in their right mind would try. His manner is smooth and silky. He tilts his head ever so slightly as his smile stretches across the entire length of his face. It practically reaches out and affectionately pulls you in. It is fascinating to watch as someone meets Max for the first time. To observe them, unaware, as they become captivated and the hook of his charm sets deeply. You can almost visibly see Max's appeal envelop and surround them. That aura spreads and begins to fill the space and veil the entire room. He has an easy way about him that is as welcome as a favorite blanket on a cold, stormy night. Max can warm the depths of a hardened heart or a weary soul with a simple glance. His naturally charismatic nature is intriguing and a truer gentleman does not exist.

Max is a Colorado boy, born in the quiet river town of Glenwood Springs on September 29, 1922. He was the fifth of six boys; Bob, Richard, John, Billy, Max and the youngest Wayne. Sadly, Max's brother Billy left this world too early at the age of two; however, the Brown house did not lack for testosterone. Max and his brother Wayne were the youngest and stuck together like peanut butter and jelly. Max's favorite memories of childhood consistently and lovingly involve Wayne.

Max's parents, William Sears Brown and Myrtle Fahl Brown were originally from Indiana. Max remembers his father as a marvelous man. He was a semi-professional baseball player, as well as a semi-professional singer and trombone player. He had a beautiful bass voice and Max remembers his father as the only man he ever knew that could do anything and everything AND do it all well.

Max tells a story about his parent's courtship. Before they were married William left Indiana and headed out West. In his absence he heard Myrtle was dating a preacher back home. To plead his case he wrapped up the head of an ax and sent it to her with a note saying she was "chopping up his heart" and with that he won her forever. There is no question where Max inherited his romantic trait.

William was a master carpenter and cabinet maker. He worked for a prominent business man named Spencer Penrose, or "Speck," as he was commonly referred to. Speck was most famous for building the world-class Broadmoor Hotel in Colorado Springs, Colorado, in 1918. Max proudly boasts that his father did the wood work around the large pillars still present in the hotel today.

William took a job with the newly formed US Forest Service. Myrtle was not thrilled with this line of work. The men were loaded on a train and transported over the Continental Divide. They then travelled the remaining six miles to the ranger station by horse and buggy. Meanwhile, Myrtle, a social person, didn't enjoy the isolation of living in the middle of a forest. However, her wish for community was soon granted. After a year with the Forest Service William was transferred to Eagle, Colorado. This was an opportune move for the Brown family as Eagle was considered a "big town" by most standards back then. It was in Eagle that Max attended his first two years of school. Bob, the oldest Brown boy had graduated and received a scholarship to the University of Colorado in Boulder and his mother was excited. This was a favorable situation for the Browns. During the winter the family would stay in Boulder, close to the schools, and then spend the summers up at the ranger station. It was the perfect scenario to keep every member of the family happy.

Max attended Whittier Elementary School in Boulder and describes the third grade as a complete disaster. He flunked the grade. The playground talk at the time was that the Principal Mrs. Fitzpatrick had an electronic spanking machine. All the children were frightened to be called to her office. However, as vivid as the image of the spanking machine was in Max's mind his school memories pale in comparison to the way he affectionately remembers the summers spent living at the ranger station. Max's father built a large porch in the back where all the boys could sleep together. It was a wonderful environment for an active, growing boy. The Brown boys would often trample down to Brush Creek and come home with buckets full of fish. That creek supplied the family with many meals over the years.

Max is full of fond summer memories especially of his adventures with his little brother Wayne. He tells of a time they met a man named Washington Hammer. Wayne and Max intimately called him "Tack" Hammer, Max recalls with a chuckle. Washington had seven or eight burros loaded down with food and supplies to be transported to the men working in the mountain mines. There was one old, lame burro that trailed behind the others and Wayne and Max instinctively felt compassion for her. Now, their father always told the boys not to borrow food or bother any of the people camping and, as a rule, the boys strictly obeyed. However, Washington offered them his camp site including some nice hot supper and, in exchange for their company, they would get to keep the lame burro.

This was quite the dilemma for the young boys but they looked at the burro as a wonderful new toy and Max recalls they couldn't resist the offer. They ate porcupine for dinner that night with Washington and it was pretty darn good. As it was beginning to get dark they scavenged around and found some wire and six to seven feet of rope and fashioned a halter. One of the boys pulled the burro from the front and the other boy pushed from behind. It took them hours to get the burro down the mountain. They named their wonderful toy Angel Face and she provided the boys with the most fun Max can remember. They hooked up inner tubes to her harness and she would pull them around. The older boys would get on her back to make her buck and even though she only had three useful legs none of them could successfully stay on.

Max recalls a time his father came running down the trail excitedly yelling to the boys to grab a horse because he had just shot a bear. Max comments at how crazy this was because his father had only a 32 caliber pistol. But then again he also had a good and fearless dog named Ole-Jim. As the story goes the bear was approximately twenty feet away when it saw William, turned and stood up to its full height. William did the only thing he could think of and that was to empty the pistol into the angry bear. Ole-Jim stayed there barking and keeping the bear down until the boys arrived with the horse and loaded it up. Max explains that bear meat isn't really too bad, but on the other hand isn't really too good either. The bear may have been a little gamey but the Browns had meat for a good long time after that.

Employing both hard work and charm, Max remembers taking some odd jobs for a little money. He cleaned up horse stables for his father's friend for a nickel. He also spent time in Estes Park, Colorado, escorting and singing for tourists on moonlight rides.

In the early 1940's William gave Max his own mare named Queenie and Max thought he had died and gone to heaven to have his very own horse. Over time though, Max moved on up to a Model-T Ford as his means of transportation. Max soon discovered that while Queenie could graze he needed money for gas if he wanted to go anywhere in a car.

About the same time Max watched as his older brother, who had joined the Colorado National Guard for college money, prepared his gear for an Annual Federal Inspection. Max figured it looked like an easy enough way to make money. Though only fifteen, he saw no reason he couldn't join too. Max, an All Conference tackle for the Boulder High School football team, stood six foot three inches and weighing in at 185 pounds. He marched into the Colorado National Guard office of Captain Roger M. Crosby and asked, "What do you have to do to join this outfit?" Captain Crosby who stood only five feet tall gazed up at Max and replied, "You're in!" He knew Max may not be old enough, but he sure was big enough!

Overall, Max enjoyed his time in the National Guard though it was a mixed bag of hard work and questionable lessons learned. As he shakes his head in near disbelief he remembers a time he was given the duty to guard the payroll overnight and while he was given a pistol, he was not given any ammunition. He chuckles as he says he never quite understood his role in protecting the payroll if someone had it in their mind to steal it.

On another assignment his unit was sent to Laramie, Wyoming, for joint training exercises with the cavalry from Cheyenne. The boys in the cavalry seemed to have a distinct advantage as they were on horseback while Max's unit crouched in trenches. The horses could simply jump right over them. In frustration Max devised a plan that involved his men shooting blanks from their weapons. The horses of course panicked and bucked. Max laughs as he admits nearly receiving a court martial for the scheme.

During another summer Max's unit went to Louisiana for training maneuvers in the back county swamps accompanied by the New Mexico National Guard. He heard a soldier shout out he'd just been bitten by a snake. The young man was already dead by the time help could reach him. Witnessing that death made an impression on the young Max even though he attempts to dismiss it now with a joke about learning the lesson of never going "swamping" again.

The threat of the war hung heavy in America as a nearly palpable sense of dread filled everyone's thoughts if not their conversations. Max wanted to join the military but Myrtle would absolutely not hear of it. She wanted her boys in college. Her desire to put off the inevitable and have Max remain in school was so strong that she marched into Captain Crosby's office and demanded Max be released as he was underage and they had no right to have him in the first place. Again, Captain Crosby acquiesced to a tough member of the Brown family, a mother raising five boys was a force to be reckoned with and Max was subsequently discharged.

Although Max and his wife-to-be Shirley both attended Colorado State University in Fort Collins they met for the first time in a fraternity house turned makeshift dance hall in Estes Park. At the time dance halls were the place to be. Everyone danced and danced well. Shirley caught Max's eye and she admits that his excellent dancing skills captured her attention as well. Max laughs that it must have been hard for her to get a good look at him through all of the girls that constantly surrounded him. But Max only had eyes for Shirley. He strolled over to her and threw out the line, "Baby where have you been all my life?" Shirley giggled and they danced together the entire night. Max stayed late to help clean up and walked Shirley home. Max describes meeting Shirley as the highlight of his life.

One spring, Max had a job shoeing horses in Estes Park. After a long day of work he drove his 1932 Desoto from Estes Park to Boulder to visit Myrtle, who was in the hospital. Mother didn't want him to make a fuss over her and assured him she was fine and sent him on his way. Max was exhausted, but figured he could manage the twenty-five mile drive back home. It turned out to be a bad decision, as nine miles up the canyon Max fell asleep at the wheel and drove the Desoto off the road.

The car crashed down a steep embankment. Max was ejected on the way and landed at the bottom in flames. He lay a few feet away, his clothes and even his boots stripped off by the fall down the hill. He lay there naked through the night, bleeding and going in and out of consciousness. Around dawn, Max forced himself awake and struggled to cling to awareness. He focused on his surroundings and managed to scrounge around and find his pants. He made several attempts to crawl up the steep hill, but the effort would strain him back into unconsciousness and send him rolling back down to the bottom.

He grew frustrated and angry at his predicament and willed himself to focus on each movement until he made it to the top of the hill. Finally, a car came down the road and Max tried to flag it down, but the driver took one look at Max; dirty, bleeding, shirtless and shoeless and sped away. Eventually, Max heard another vehicle approaching and in a desperate act of sheer determination he stood right in the middle of the road. The driver of an early morning bread truck stopped and gave Max a ride back to town. Max boasts that he was patched up and back to work shoeing horses again the very next day.

In spite of his less than stellar driving record, Max soon found work driving a Yellow cab for a little extra money. Max was on the job the morning of December 7, 1941, his fare was a couple of elderly ladies on their way to church. As the news of the Japanese bombing of Pearl Harbor echoed from the radio it immediately stifled the air in the cab as time stood still.

Max was enrolled in the V12 Marine Corps program in college, but he no longer wanted to go to school. He wanted to go to war. Max had already experienced the Army through his stint in the National Guard. There was a mystique about the Marines and the valor and fame of the recent battle for Guadalcanal Island brought the fascination of the Corps to the forefront. Max wanted to be a Marine. Everyone did.

It wasn't long before Max found himself in sunny San Diego, California, standing on the legendary painted yellow foot prints in formation in United States Marine Corps boot camp. Marine recruits west of the Mississippi River attended boot camp in San Diego while recruits east of the Mississippi reported to the famous Parris Island. Max thought boot camp was a snap. He found that his National Guard training served him well and he graduated with honors.

Eight weeks later he became a drill instructor himself. If pressed, he would describe himself as a firm, but never mean, drill instructor. He takes satisfaction, to this day, that he feels he turned out some really good Marines. He hopes the lessons he taught helped save some lives during the war. Max served fourteen months as a drill instructor and says it was his favorite job in the Corps. The boys were so young and many did not even know why they were there. Max explained that all young people need vision and it was both an honor and a responsibility to help give them focus.

He was eventually transferred to Camp Pendleton where he learned to fire and field strip every single weapon the Marine Corps had. From there, in September 1944, he was sent to Maui, Hawaii, and joined the 4th Marine Division. While in Maui he served guard duty and basically did whatever tasks needed to be done.

One day in Maui after hours of battling large brush fires ignited from their training maneuvers, Max and a few other Marines decided to head down to the beach to clean-up and cool off in the ocean. They took turns throwing each other up and into the water. Just to show off Max performed a superb back lay out, but the water was too shallow and he hit hard when he landed. His companions were sure his neck had been broken. He was treated in Sick Bay and was forced to wear a neck brace collar. Max's neck improved little over time and remained weak. The discs in his neck were ultimately fused years later.

From Maui Max boarded a ship bound for the island of Iwo Jima. They were on the ship for three days when the brass invited the Marines to the deck and explained the mission using a mockup of Iwo Jima Island. They were allowed to ask any and all questions they had, however, the answer was always the same, "We don't know." No one had any idea what to expect. The scenarios ranged from "over in a few days" to "the most horrific battle ever." Iwo Jima is not a very large island so the Marines believed that the possibility still existed that it could be captured quickly. Max recalled he had absolutely no idea what to expect and couldn't even begin to imagine.

Before the final leg of the voyage to Iwo Jima, the ship docked at an island and the Marines were allowed liberty. Max had an excruciating headache, almost to the point of vomiting and so he never left the ship. He felt his head was going to burst. He had never before or ever since had a headache like that one. He can only attribute it to the stress and anxiety of the pending mission. Upon approach of the island as Iwo Jima came into view against the horizon the sheer number of vessels in the water was awe inspiring. The small island was surrounded by nearly 800 ships of every conceivable shape and size. Max knew then that capturing the island quickly was beyond hope.

Max was a replacement Marine. As a replacement he stood at the ready waiting to take the place of a fallen Marine. No words can fully describe the torment and apprehension of watching the battle for two and a half days from the deck of the ship. He listened to the intense, seemingly unending bombing, waiting cruelly for his turn. He watched as planes dove in and disappeared behind clouds of black smoke and billowing dust. He would feel sickened with the thought of the crash just as the plane would miraculously reappear through the haze, victorious. He watched in awe as this occurred over and over.

Max witnessed the famous flag rising on Mount Suribachi from the deck of the ship. It was a wonderful sight and an overwhelming experience as all the surrounding ships sounded their sirens, fired flares and shot off the guns. He could hear the men on the island hooting and hollering as everything seemed to go crazy. The high ground had been captured and winning the battle was now only a matter of time. It wasn't until the fourth day, D-Day plus 4, that Max descended the dreaded cargo net into the Higgins boat below and headed for the beach. He focused and thought to himself, *well, this is it. I will do the best I can.*

The Higgins boat tossed and pitched violently as it headed into shore. Some lost the contents of their stomachs. They couldn't get close enough for a normal beach ascent because of the equipment and casualties in the water. They were forced to exit the vessel into the now blood soaked ocean, with rough water up to their necks, struggling to hold their rifles above their heads. Bodies, parts of bodies and equipment floated around in the churning sea. It was a horrific sight. Bulldozers on the beach simply tried to push everything out of the way. Fires burned. Bombs exploded. The scene was complete chaos. The black, volcanic sand seemed to swallow everything. It was loose and always moving, swirling around. It was a fifty yard gauntlet up to the next level where Max dug a foxhole as best he could in the unforgiving sand and waited until a man went down and a replacement was called for.

The call came and Max dodged and raced up a trail until he reached his new squad. He was introduced to the only two Marines left in it. The captain quickly filled the three men in on their mission. He ordered them to head over to a large, thirty foot high, concrete structure. They were to figure out what it was and report back. Max said, "Okay men, let's head over there."

The first man replied back to Max, "No way! I'm not going with you!"

The second Marine said, "Nor am I!"

They felt it was a suicide mission. They had no cover fire for protection because there were no men left in their squad. The Japanese had trap doors all over the island. They could pop up anywhere, at any time, and take a Marine out in an instant. To Max it was simple; the work needed to be done and so he would do it. Max shrugged them off and went alone. Max suspected he looked like the fictional character Ichabod Crane from *The Legend of Sleepy Hollow*. He was tall and lanky, uncoordinated as he ran as fast as he could dodging and zigzagging because his life depended on it. He arrived panting and out of breath, but happy to have made it to his objective successfully. He poked around and sure enough, had no idea what it was. He concluded it was possibly a water reservoir the Japanese had constructed. Max explained how uniquely disciplined the Japanese soldiers were and clarified their tactics. While he was on the jog of his life there was a machine gun nest to the left, but the Japanese soldiers were given precise fields of fire and would not think of deviating from their instructions. They could have easily cut Max down, but didn't because he was not in their range of order. He owed his life to their discipline and strategy. He did another Ichabod Crane imitation to get back to safety and reported that he honestly didn't know what it was, possibly a water tank. On the surface it didn't appear Max accomplished much on this mission, but actually he did. He proved himself to the men and he earned their respect. They never again questioned another order and did whatever Max requested of them.

A few days later there was an intense fire fight. Marines were getting hit and going down all around. A grenade exploded behind Max riddling him with shrapnel and blowing out both of his ear drums. Bleeding profusely from the wounds in his back and with blood streaming from both his ears, time seemed in slow motion, his head filled with ringing as he felt the fog and haze of confusion closing in on him. He called for the Navy corpsmen. A corpsman dropped into his foxhole and pulled some of the shrapnel out of his back, patching him up as best he could. He told Max to head for the beach and report to the hospital ship. Max didn't want to go back, he wanted to continue on and stay in the battle. It was part of the corpsmen's job to fill out a register documenting the specifics of each soldier treated. The corpsman who treated Max was immediately killed when he left Max's foxhole so there was no official record of the incident. The shrapnel is still in Max's back today and he remains dependent upon hearing aids.

Max says they rarely saw the Japanese soldiers and when they did catch a glimpse they appeared to be impossibly young. Max swears some were not more than twelve-years-old. He spent a total of thirty-six days and nights on the island of Iwo Jima with most of it blurred together leaving him with only bits and pieces of distinct recollections. At one point he found a Japanese battle flag, two beautiful swords and a Japanese pistol. For a while he tried to carry them around thinking he could take them home someday but it seemed every time he turned around he hit someone with them and they were a hassle to lug. He made the decision to bury the souvenirs thinking he would return and dig them up before he left the island. He marked the spot and knew exactly where he left them. Unfortunately, when he returned to the location he found only a brand new runway lay completely covering the area.

The Marines spent their last days on the island walking around poking in holes and recovering weapons. There was still sporadic gunfire on the far end of the island when suddenly they saw a young Japanese soldier dart into a crevice. One of the Marines was carrying a shake charge. Without warning or explanation he pulled the pin and threw the entire briefcase sized explosive into the crevice. To this day, in his recurring nightmares, Max still clearly sees the image of that Japanese soldier's perfectly formed spinal column flying into the air. Max could not understand why that Marine let his emotions get the best of him. There was absolutely no reason for his actions. To see, up close, a fatal example of man's inhumanity to man was devastating.

Before leaving Iwo Jima the Marines buried the last of their buddies and spent time wandering through the graves looking for the names of friends. It was a heartbreaking ritual, but somehow necessary. They were emotionally and physically exhausted. The air was as thick and heavy as their hearts, almost as if the sorrow and loss could actually be felt or breathed. Max found the grave of his first drill instructor, Max Wagner. Wagner, in life, had been a beautiful man and a real Marine's Marine. Max was saddened to leave him there. The battle had taken the man who had taught him the skills he needed to survive it.

Two days later they were finally loaded on transports and taken to the ships to leave. Max was thankful he didn't have to wade through chest-deep water as he had, a lifetime ago, when they arrived. Although filled with men the ship was quiet as the joy of survival met with a bottomless sense of loss; loss of their friends, loss of their innocence, loss of their youth; loss of themselves.

The Marines headed back to Maui to continue their training and prepare for the planned invasion of mainland Japan. Predictions called for a ninety-five percent loss and all warnings forecasted nothing short of a blood bath was to be expected. They set up mock towns to train and focused on the immeasurable task that lay ahead, not because it seemed possible but because it simply had to be done. You could hear, see, and feel the collective sigh of relief when in August the loudspeakers broadcast the end of the war. No one sums up the war's end better than Max when he says, "It felt like ice cream every day!"

Many Marines were able to head home. Max was two points short and found himself walking up a gangplank to board a ship bound for China. Someone conducted a last minute recount and called out Max's name. Not waiting to hear it twice he tossed his sea bag over the side and jumped off the plank with a thud. He was home in time for Christmas 1945.

William went alone to pick up his son at the train station in Denver. He told Myrtle he wanted to be the one to bring his son home. With wet eyes and a lump in his throat Max struggles today to describe how his normally stoic father swallowed him up and hugged the breath out of him with unashamed tears streaming down his face.

He soon learned that his dear little brother Wayne had been killed in Italy while he had been fighting in Iwo Jima. Wayne was in the 10th Mountain Division. He was a Browning automatic weapon man and had wiped out three machine gun nests before being cut down. Wayne's letters home described the Army's role in Italy at the time as "not very active" while it was clear that Max was headed to the Pacific for a major offensive.

When the telegram arrived Myrtle could barely get the words to escape her lips as she whispered, "It's Max isn't it?"

William's eyes locked with hers as he quietly responded, "No, it's Wayne."

Wayne Brown was laid to rest in the Florence American Cemetery and Memorial in Florence, Italy. A beautiful seventy acre site on a hillside that Max and his wife Shirley would eventually have the opportunity to visit in 1965. Though given the option to bring Wayne's body home his family decided he should remain with the people he fought with and the people he fought for.

Throughout his enlistment Max and Shirley exchanged beautiful and steamy letters. Shirley would pour her heart out to Max in her letters while he would write back telling her not to worry because someday they would tell their grandchildren about it. Shirley knew then that Max's intentions were honorable. Shirley wanted to do her part for her country so she joined the Marines as well. She served the Corps at Camp Lejeune, North Carolina, and at Parris Island, South Carolina. Shirley was an only child and was blessed to have a family that supported her in the Marines. A service flag was displayed in the window of their home and people would say to her father, "Hey Gordie, do you have a son in the Army?"

Her father would proudly bellow back in reply, "No, a daughter in the Marines!"

Life after the war was such a happy time. Everyone appreciated and enjoyed the simple things in life because they had done without so much. It seemed as if everyone was getting married. Life was grand and with the return of the men the dance halls were open again. Shirley was having fun. So, Shirley said to Max, "I hope you don't mind but there are a lot of guys to date right now." She returned his fraternity pin, which was a symbol of an engagement to be engaged.

Max, a little hurt by her actions, replied, "Well, alright but you are going to have to beg me for it back."

Shirley went on a date to a dance with another young man even though Max had asked for a date the same night. The other guy was a terrible dancer and Shirley was not impressed. She realized she was being ridiculous and that she really just wanted to be with Max. She also overheard another girl talking about how she thought Max was cute and Shirley knew that if Max went on a date with someone else she could never live with herself.

She made a decision and borrowed her father's car. She raced over and picked up Max. She stopped the car near some railroad tracks where it was dark and quiet, switched off the ignition, turned to him and said, "So when are we going to get married?" They were married quite appropriately on June 14, 1946, Flag Day.

They began their lives together living in a two bedroom Quonset hut. Both used their G.I. Bill to once again attend Colorado State University in Fort Collins. In 1949 their son Gordon William Brown, named for each of their fathers, was born.

At a luncheon in downtown Denver Max thought he recognized a man sitting across the table. He was trying to puzzle it out when the man suddenly said, "Were you in the Marine Corps?" Max realized that the man had been a colonel with the 4th Marine Division. Still in the Corps, he explained to Max that the Marines were in the process of forming a gun battalion and that he could assist Max in gaining a commission. Getting back in the Corps sounded very appealing to Max and with talk of another war brewing in Korea he knew he would end up answering the call once again anyway so why not make more money as a commissioned officer.

Max returned to the Corps by February, 1950, and war in Korea was declared the following June. Again he found himself on a ship heading into battle. He landed at Inchon on August 2. They accomplished their mission of taking and securing the airport. They boarded the ship once again and headed north where they established a beach head in Wonsan.

During mail call, while in North Korea, Max received a letter from the Commandant of the United States Marine Corps thanking him for his exemplary record, but denying him access back into the Corps because of his age. Apparently they thought he was too old for the rigors of battle at the ripe old age of twenty-eight. Max chuckled at the irony and still has the actual letter.

Although times in Korea were hard and the conditions were harsh, Max always kept his optimism and sense of humor. He did his part to keep spirits up, and achieved a certain amount of fame, by making great apple dumplings from scrounged supplies and an oven made of rocks. With his famous smile, Max recalls another time when they had set up a perimeter and left a young Marine from St. Louis on night watch with a 50 caliber weapon. They were all startled awake by the sound of opening fire. They ran over and he was as white as a sheet, shaking. He tried to convince them that although he had completely missed it there really was a huge tiger. The Marines, of course, teased him although they did find the fresh, gigantic tracks of a Siberian tiger the next morning.

Max remained stationed at the base of the Chosin Reservoir and wasn't personally involved in one of the most famous battles in Marine Corps history and the history of the Korean War; the Chosin Reservoir Campaign. The 1st Marine Division was cut off from support due to the worst weather conditions in fifty years. It was snowing and windy with temperatures registering a frigid forty degrees below zero. Though surrounded and through the harshest of circumstances, the Marines successfully defeated ten Chinese Infantry Divisions despite the odds. The Marines of that excruciating brutal battle are affectionately referred to as "The Chosin Few" and will forever remain revered.

One night Max sat at the camp fire and smelled something burning only to realize it was his own fingers. The shrapnel in his back had caused nerve damage and he had lost feeling in his fingers. He was transported to a hospital on the Japanese mainland and from there spent six months at a naval hospital in Oakland, California, where he was officially discharged from the Corps.

Max feels truly blessed having been born an American and into a family that loved and cherished him. William was his guidepost and compass while Myrtle instilled faith and love deep in his heart. Max is most proud of his marriage to Shirley. Through the good and the rough patches he is proud of what they did together. With the exception of losing their son Gordon to a car accident in 1970 Max speaks of the many blessings he has enjoyed throughout his life. Their daughter Christine was born in 1951 and with her marriage to their wonderful son-in-law Max feels that although he lost a son he gained a new one along with two beautiful granddaughters. Max's promise to Shirley had been kept. There are so many stories to tell the grandchildren.

Max defines courage as the ability to do something that's for the best even though it's difficult or dangerous. He sees a narrow line between foolishness and bravery and admits he's been on both sides. Max credits his family and his childhood at the ranger station with inspiring much of his character as an adult. He had the guts to endure Iwo Jima because he was taught that you do whatever needs to be done regardless of how difficult it is. If it has to be done, you do it. It's that simple.

It wasn't until 2008 that Max finally received the medals he was due. At a Veteran's Day Ceremony with his family, friends and other assorted fans in attendance he was awarded the Bronze Star, the Purple Heart, the Combat Action Ribbon, the Navy Presidential Unit Citation, the Marine Corps Good Conduct Medal, the American Defense Service, the Asiatic Pacific Campaign, the World War II Victory ribbon, the Korean Service and Korean Defense Service ribbon, the Marine Corps Drill Instructor ribbon, the Republic of Korea Presidential Unit Citation and the United Nations Service ribbon.

Max stood on the stage that day so tall and proud. You could clearly see the Marine still present in his eighty-year-old body. As I watched him my vision was clouded by tears of appreciation and respect. I felt that finally everyone could see the complete man and Marine, the Max that I see. To me, those awards were a tangible symbol, a testament to the man and a representation of his character, spirit and soul. Although he felt he didn't need medals on his chest to prove anything it felt good to be honored and recognized by the country and Corps to which he dedicated most of his life.

Max enjoys speaking to groups of school-age children because he believes future generations need to establish goals for themselves; hard, ambitious goals. He feels young people today are so intelligent and capable with the possibility of enormous potential if they don't limit themselves. He encourages the children to never give up, to just do it. He tells them to dream, and dream big, but also to create a concrete plan to achieve their dreams. He wants them to understand that even though it is not going to be easy they should do it anyway because it matters that you don't give up. Max's message resonates because his life and his character provide a living breathing example of focus, belief, determination and spirit.

What I admire most about Max Brown is his gentle humility. He has a calm, unassuming, accepting nature that finds the good in everyone. It is easy to appreciate what a good Marine, drill instructor, friend, husband, father and grandfather he was and is. He has the ability to look into your eyes and your heart and see a great future, a future that exists if only you can believe in yourself like he already believes in you. Max could convince an angel to leave heaven. He has a gift for finding your essence, your best, your potential and drawing it out like a magnet. He lures it out from your soul and as it seems to just unravel and flow so easily from within you, it makes you wonder why you kept it all wound up so tight inside you in the first place. Just knowing Max Brown makes you fearless.

In the silence I let out the breath I didn't realize I had been holding. None of us had even moved the entire time Max relayed his experiences. We were all captivated, frozen by his charm and his story. I wince with a slight pain in my side as I lean back into the support of my chair apparently oblivious to the tension in my body as I clung to his words.

As I start to relax I glance over at the final Marine seated at our table, Jim Blane. The word that comes to mind is class. Jim is a man of few words but when he does speak it is in your best interest to pay close attention.

He eases back in his chair, crosses his arms and takes in a slow, deep breath. He looks around the table at each one of our expectant faces. There are so many different emotions that flicker across his face; pain, sorrow, sadness, compassion, understanding yet there are many more that I cannot comprehend, although I sense that they do not escape the other men's attention. There is an unspoken bond of empathy. We wait. Jim seems hesitant, it's as if he is not sure where to begin or even how to begin. But he takes one last glimpse down, flicks a small piece of lint from his pants and begins to tell his story.

Max, Drill Instructor (right)

A young Max

Shirley, in her Marine uniform

Shirley, skiing

Shirley and Max, just married

Max still looks at Shirley the same way today

February 4, 1945
At Sea

My Dearest One,

I'm sorry that you haven't recieved more mail from me but as you will soon see — it really couldn't be helped. Now it can be told or at least partly revealed — I am aboard a transport and on my merry way into combat. Our days are filled with lectures on the coming operation and of the things we can expect. Then, of course, there are the card games and physical exercises, etc. The chow is swell and, so far, we've had lots of water for showers. We get our laundry done in the ships laundry and have access to the ships store. So you see, we are living

A letter from Max to Shirley on the ship to Iwo Jima

fairly comfortable. Everyone seems to be in good spirit and more or less looking forward for the things to come. I can't say that I'm totally happy about it all but I'm not afraid. I don't know what to be afraid of. It might be different if I had been in combat before. Somehow, I feel that everything will be O.K., so don't worry, please. We aren't allowed to say anymore about the operation and besides, by the time you recieve this you will have read all about it in the newspapers. Of course, later on, I will be able to tell little details that are strictly forbidden now. Then maybe I can tell about where we have been since coming overseas and some of the things I've seen. It has really been quite interesting.

Precious, my every hour has been filled

with thoughts of you. I sleep out on the deck at nite and look at the beautiful stars and think of you, my star. I love you so very much that, at times, I feel as if I must burst. It is such a wonderful feeling and yet I long so much to see you and hold you close to me that it hurts me. You are so dear to me. I want so badly to say these things to you personally and back in cool, colorful, Colorado but that is impossible so I have to use this means of conveying my feelings. No matter what happens, I want you to know that I hold you more precious than anything I know. Believe me! I've thought it all out. It has been so long since we've seen each other and everything has been so happenstance and so distant and yet after studying all angles I'm sure beyond a doubt that you were meant to be mine. I can't fail with such a destiny.

Several of the guys have threatened my life and everything else if I don't send their love to you and I'm the jealous type, too but I do love life. Your are quite the favorite with them — and me too! So I'll just say "Hello!" from the whole outfit.

Gee, there isn't much more I can say and this will be the last letter I can write for some time to come. That hurts. So long for awhile precious. I'll being thinking of you as always

All my love, all my life

As Ever

Max

Jim Blane

Patriotism is not short, frenzied outbursts of emotion,
but the tranquil and steady dedication of a lifetime.
— Adlai E. Stevenson

Jim Blane is the father-figure at the table. He is respected by all, even revered. He is not someone you want to disappoint. It is not a role he wanted necessarily, but he has come to accept it. Jim is a small-framed man, but I have an image in my mind of his ribcage bowing out, struggling to contain and protect an unusually large heart. He enjoys assisting fellow veterans and helping them navigate the maze of available benefits.

Jim carries a serious, almost heavy expression that can be misunderstood upon first meeting him. It is a reflection of Jim merely actively contemplating what tasks he can accomplish and looking forward to the next big challenge to conquer. He is organized and efficient. Without fanfare or self-aggrandizement of any kind he gets involved and gets things done. Though soft-spoken he can easily control a room and people naturally look to him for direction. He is level-headed yet compassionate. He just wants to make sure everyone is taken care of properly.

Jim attempts to speak in his usual stern, business-like manner, but he is noticeably uncomfortable and his discomfort is felt by everyone at the table. The other men know, and I can only guess, at the demons he has battled for the past sixty-five years. Jim is currently working with a therapist at the VA Hospital, and perhaps because he is finally working through the repressed issues that he is able to summon his usual calm, no-nonsense demeanor this morning. He has put on his game-face too many times and paid the price. Jim has weathered some truly rough times, even by the standards of other battle-tested Marines, and has seen the ugliest side of mankind. With all that the experiences have taken from him, insight and wisdom remain in equal measure.

Jim was born at home during a wicked ice storm in Mason City, Illinois, on November 18, 1924. He was the first child for Arthur Millard and Gladys Blane. He slept comfortably in a dresser drawer his parents used as a bassinet. Jim joked that when he cried or fussed his parents probably simply shut the drawer. Gladys and Arthur

Millard, affectionately known as "Milky," were no strangers to hardship and the necessity of making do with what they had, as both their families had originally migrated to the United States from Ireland to escape the potato famine. While Milky had never finished high school, his bride, Gladys Hughes, had been school president during her senior year and her classmates nicknamed her "Happy" which was entirely appropriate. There weren't many jobs in Mason City for Milky who was trained as a mechanic, so the young family moved to Peoria, Illinois, in search of better opportunities. Milky eventually found work as a butcher. Two years later Jim's little brother Robert arrived to complete the Blane family.

Jim describes a happy childhood growing up in Peoria. After a few years Gladys needed to go back to work and had to find a place for her two young sons during the day. Rather resourcefully, she lied about Jim's age to enroll him in kindergarten a year early and effectively cut her daycare expenses in half. The ruse worked out well for Jim as he thrived in school. He made many friends and excelled in athletics. He played basketball and golf, as well as ran track. He chuckles as he explains that he was also on the football team for exactly one day. On the first day of practice, Jim arrived late so the coach kicked him off the team. He thought that decision turned out to be in his best interests as with many circumstances in his life. The protective equipment for football players in those days was minimal and many players on the team suffered serious injuries. Jim now believes the coach did him a favor.

The high school had fraternities and sororities similar to the college environment today. Jim belonged to the most popular fraternity and his steady girlfriend belonged to the most popular sorority. They were quite an "item" and graduated in 1942. Jim's girlfriend attended college while he took a job at the Central Illinois Light Company. He was paid $17.50 a week and provided a bus pass.

Jim, along with two other young men, hand delivered light bills door-to-door. Each was responsible for a third of the residences in the city. They delivered the bills as fast as possible, not because they were particularly industrious, but because any free working time was devoted to relaxation and shooting pool. Jim was so fast at working his territory that he became quite good at pool and still gives billiard lessons today. It wasn't long before Jim was promoted to mail boy with the responsibility of delivering mail to the executive offices and picking up any outgoing mail. Soon, he was promoted again to printing machine operator. Jim printed the bills he had once hand delivered.

Jim and three of his friends registered for the draft as required in 1942. They discussed their options and all agreed they preferred a better assignment than the Army and so the decision was made to join the United States Marine Corps together. Jim had been just a junior in high school when Pearl Harbor was bombed. Hawaii was a long way from mid-western Illinois and seemed like a different country altogether. The world was a smaller place in the 1940s, without television or the internet, but it was about to expand dramatically for the three young men as they were officially sworn into the Marines on March 1, 1943.

Their journey started with a long train ride from Chicago to San Diego by way of El Paso, Texas, and San Francisco. Boot camp in San Diego was typical of Marine Corps lore. The young men were forced to stand at attention on the yellow painted footprints while they were screamed at, harassed and otherwise tortured to the breaking point. Jim enjoyed most of boot camp and did well. It could be that boot camp is comparable to child birth for women, the pain and discomfort fades over time and one is left with a sense of accomplishment and an appreciation for the lasting imprint the experience placed on your life and on your soul.

Jim and two of his friends were assigned to Platoon 230 where they had exceptional drill instructors. One in particular, Corporal Green, made a lasting impression on Jim. Most drill instructors were a version of the stereotype – obscenities screamed inches from the face, spit flew with every word, and veins protruded from the temples of their red faces. Corporal Green, however, did not fit the stereotype. In fact, he was the exact opposite. He never raised his voice. He was the type of leader that didn't have to. He had "the look" and it would make your knees buckle. He demanded and commanded respect. In listening to Jim characterize Corporal Green it strikes me that Jim is really describing himself without realizing it.

Part of the unique experience of boot camp was life in close quarters with people of different backgrounds and circumstances, some quite different from your own. The young men grew up in basically homogeneous communities. The majority of families had immigrated to America from other countries and settled together forming neighborhoods. Boot camp had a way of quickly broadening experiences and teaching the men how to live with, and accept one another.

In the chow hall one day a Platoon 230 recruit from New York requested his hamburger remain uncooked. Jim was shocked when he proceeded to eat the patty raw and seemed to enjoy it. Over time, Jim grew to enjoy rare meat and laughs as he remembers the Irish culinary example set by his parents. On occasion Jim's father the butcher would bring home a beautiful, juicy cut of filet mignon. His mother would slice off a thick piece and they would proceed to flatten it with a cleaver and cook it to death – basically ruining a choice cut of beef.

In boot camp one night the recruits were issued ammunition and quickly transported to the shore and ordered to dig foxholes. They spent a long, vigilant night on the beach. Apparently, there had been a threat of a possible Japanese invasion, but as daylight broke all was well and the men soon found themselves back on base returning their ammo. The recruits were perplexed by this episode, but they quickly shrugged it off as they were becoming accustomed to a dearth of information and they went back to training as usual as if nothing had happened.

It was very cold on the rifle range at Camp Mathews and Jim quickly learned how to use newspapers as insulation to keep warm. He worked at the range pulling down the used targets and replacing them with new, fresh sheets. At the time no type of ear protection existed and Jim started to notice a ringing in his ears later diagnosed as tinnitus. It was, and still is, an affliction without a cure. Jim's tinnitus has progressively worsened over the years and has been especially difficult when he tries to sleep. He found some relief from the ringing with a sound machine that peacefully emits ocean and rainforest sounds so he can rest.

Maintaining peace in both his head and his heart prove to be a continuing effort in his life.

It was an almost unprecedented event when all of Platoon 230 graduated from boot camp together. No recruit failed, was injured or washed out.

Stationed in Camp Elliot, just south of Camp Pendleton, California, Jim started his military career as an office clerk. He lived in the barracks at night and ran the duplicating machine during the day. The machine was basically a big drum, sticky with ink. Jim would turn a large crank and the drum would turn, transferring the image to one piece of paper after another. As the only independently moving part, Jim was essentially the motor of the copy machine. Jim took the monotonous work in stride until he was replaced by a woman Marine (referred to as a "WM") and sent to join the 20th Engineering Regiment in Camp Pendleton where he lived with the Navy Seabees.

The Seabees were skilled members of the Navy Construction Battalion renowned for their construction and reconstruction efforts, especially during times of war. The Seabees were instrumental in the success of World War II's Pacific 'Island Hopping' campaign through their construction and paving of roadways and airstrips.

The members of the Engineering Battalion were a montage of specialists including geologists, ordinance experts and construction managers. All of the members were older and better educated than Jim. However, Jim had a skill no other member of the Battalion possessed – he could type. Jim handled all of the office work. He had learned to type in high school because he could not read his own handwriting. He chuckles that he never minded a bit being the only boy in a female typing class. It had been a survival skill in high school but, as it turned out, it helped during the war and may very well have saved Jim's life.

The men of the Engineering Battalion trained together on maneuvers, hiking and simulating beach landings on Catalina Island. They practiced climbing up and down the ship's rope ladders again and again. In January 1944 they joined the 4th Marine Division and boarded the U.S.S. Typhoon headed for Maui where they anchored off shore, but were not allowed to leave the ship. Once again they were given no information and Jim can only assume they took on supplies. The 4th Marine Division was the first in history to head directly from the states to the battlefield. They were part of "Operation Flintlock," an offensive strike that would attempt to gain a foothold in enemy territory. The Island Hopping campaign of World War II began with the objective of securing a strategic airfield.

The target was the small island of Roi-Namur located on the northern section of the Marshall Islands. Roi-Namur was actually two small islands connected by a man-made causeway and hosted a small native population. When they reached the island, only the commanding officer, his body guard and Jim boarded the Higgins boat and went ashore. Jim was never quite clear on why the three of them went in first and the rest of the unit came in later.

The unit was comprised of only support troops with no assault troops. The mission for the Navy Seabees was to construct the airfield while the rest of the men located and dismantled landmines, took prisoners and basically improvised whatever work was necessary to ensure the successful completion of the airfield. During the battle for

Roi-Namur the men had their first encounter with the "Japanese Marines," the special landing force for the Imperial Navy.

Physically they were very impressive in comparison to the other Japanese the men had encountered. They were tall and very muscular, weighing over two hundred pounds which was distinctive for the culture.

As the men went about the work of securing the island and constructing the airfield the initial shock of war poured over them like a dark, looming wave in an angry ocean. They were unprepared for the experience because no training, no maneuver, no simulated battle can prepare a man for the experience of war. Jim watched as his closest buddy went down on that beach and he could do nothing but watch powerlessly. He was dead within seconds and those precious seconds defined the reality of war for Jim.

In retrospect, Jim felt he handled himself well and tried to find something, anything, positive to focus on. He was the youngest of the men and had the fewest responsibilities and no dependents worrying and waiting back home. He felt sorry for the married men, especially the ones with children, and the extra weight that placed on them. Jim particularly held admiration for the squad leader, John Ryan. John was slightly older and offered his support and guidance generously to the others. It was a maturing experience to say the least and despite the circumstances they were a cohesive unit and enjoyed each other's company.

Away from the base, Jim migrated from clerk to company "gopher." As the youngest and least educated of the group he was given all of the nastiest, most unpopular jobs no one else wanted. On the island this consisted of hauling explosives to the front lines; retrieving unexploded ordinance; removing ammunition, grenades, rifles and hand weapons from the fallen; transporting replacement flame thrower tanks; and working the "body detail." This regrettable assignment involved transporting bodies and in some cases, body parts to the designated burial area. Jim would find himself stuck with this particular assignment for the remainder of the war and many times while under direct fire.

Similar to his experience getting kicked off the high school football team, Jim would again come to realize that what initially seemed like an unfortunate turn of events may have, in the end, saved him from something far worse. Jim was busy in the cemetery on body detail when the second largest explosion in the history of the Pacific occurred when the ammo dump was hit by a 20mm shell. Twelve men were killed in the tremendous explosion, but the cemetery was far enough away that Jim was spared. The ammo dump was full of trinitrotoluene, more commonly known as the explosive TNT, which came in eight inch by six inch by two inch blocks. Later estimates indicated that three to four tons of TNT exploded creating a crater forty feet deep. Being at sea-level the crater immediately filled with water becoming one muddy, bloody, horrific and debris filled water pit.

The island of Roi-Namur was taken in just a week though every minute of every day lasted an eternity. The Marines left, turning the job of occupation over to the Army. They buried their dead, loaded the casualties on the ship and headed back to Hawaii; much different from the men they had been seven days ago.

Upon their return to Camp Maui, the men went back to living in tents and again assumed their regular duties. Jim returned to his office work as the company clerk and it was back to business as usual. They still practiced jungle maneuvers, but now with the hearts and minds of seasoned combat veterans. They trained the new replacements, but Jim preferred not to get acquainted with the new guys. It was just easier if you didn't get to know them on a personal level. It's common human nature to protect body, mind and spirit in this manner.

In stark contrast to the reputation of hard-drinking, bar-hopping Marines on liberty, Jim and his buddies didn't drink. They preferred to trade their allowance of two beer tickets for candy bars. Jim never had a drop of alcohol while in the service, though unfortunately would eventually find his way to alcohol as a means of pushing away the dark, painful, haunting experiences of the war. On May 4, 1944, the 4th Marine Division heeded the call and loaded up again to head to Saipan. This time they were accompanied by the 2nd Marine Division and the 27th Army Division.

When the ship reached Saipan, Jim was the first to disembark and head down the rope to the Higgins boat transport below. The first three Marines down were to steady the rope ladder for the rest, protecting them from broken bones as the ship swayed while the Higgins boat bounced like a cork in the rough sea. Jim didn't have that protection and on the way down he lost his grip and fell. The Higgins boat was on an up swell in the sea and he was coming down with an additional seventy pounds of gear. He hit the boat hard twisted on his side and injured his shoulder, hip and knee. Looking back, Jim is sure that without his helmet he would not have survived the fall. A corpsman gave Jim some pills to dull the pain and gave him the option to return to the ship. Jim knew the war wasn't stopping for any man and he didn't want to be left behind, so with the invincibility reserved for the young he loaded up his gear and trudged on.

Saipan was more jungle terrain than Roi-Namur and had a much larger native population. By the time the Americans arrived the natives had already been enslaved by occupying Japanese soldiers. The native men and boys were used as labor and the women as concubines. As badly as the natives were treated by the Japanese they were led to believe it would be worse if they were captured by the Americans. As the Marines gained ground and pushed the Japanese deeper into the jungle, it was easy for the natives to believe the soldier's propaganda.

Now the official company gopher, Jim was getting pretty good at doing whatever needed to be done. One of the duties of Jim's unit was converting sea water into potable water. They had portable desalinization units that had long suction hoses that were placed in the ocean.

Water from the hoses would be processed through the units to remove the salt and create water fit for human consumption. Although there were two fresh water lakes on Saipan the desalinization units were needed as well to keep up the supply of this precious commodity. Jim was constantly hauling more water, ammunition and gear to the front lines as the need for all was relentless. If he had any spare time, it was spent with the demolition team and the flame throwers sealing the islands many caves.

One day, Jim's commanding officer noticed an Amtrak vehicle just off shore that had been abandoned for days. As it didn't appear to be damaged, the CO yelled at Jim to get his butt out there and evaluate to see if there was anything of value to recover. Jim was not particularly happy about the assignment, but such is the life of the company gopher. Jim waded out into the surf and when the water reached his chest, he swam, eventually reaching the stranded Amtrak.

Slippery and wet, he boosted himself up and out of the water and climbed onboard. As he opened the hatch, instinct took over before his mind could process the grisly scene and he flung himself backwards, nearly falling back into the water. The Amtrak's driver was still in his seat, he lifeless hands clenching the controls. His head had been severed clean from his body by a 20mm shell that had penetrated the small port that functioned as the vehicle's viewing window. The image of the headless, bloated body along with the smell of this disturbing event remains vividly etched in Jim's mind sixty-five years later.

Other unsettling memories of Saipan linger as well, and Jim struggled to find words to describe them. Many of the island's natives did eventually escape from the Japanese Army and made their way through the jungle, their desperation being stronger than their apprehension of the Americans. Jim can only guess they were willing to take their chances with the unknown rather than the horrors of the known with their present captors.

They would emerge from the jungle with nothing; broken, dirty, hungry and tired. Most of them had no shoes or clothing. One day, as Jim paused to open and eat his C-Rations a young boy, maybe five-years-old, appeared through the foliage. A naked woman, cradling an infant, slowly appeared a few feet behind him. Not knowing exactly what to do, Jim held out a piece of candy for the small child. The boy crept forward and timidly took the candy from Jim's hand and at the same time started to sob. The boy suddenly slung out his tiny skinny arms and latched on around Jim's leg and refused to let go. It was heart-breaking to see the desperation in his eyes and the eyes of his mother, but in retrospect they were some of the most fortunate of the natives.

The north side of the island had a sheer cliff face that dropped sharply into the rough sea below. As the Marines continued to close in on the Japanese, and ultimately victory, the Japanese began to realize the hopelessness of their resistance. The Japanese, as a culture, viewed surrender as disgraceful, leaving the alternative of death the more honorable choice. Few took this definition of honor more seriously than the Japanese Army and the natives of Saipan.

The Marines watched in horror, helpless, as the Japanese hurled themselves off the cliffs into the unforgiving waters far below. Babies and children pleaded and begged, but were pushed and thrown to their deaths by their parents who soon followed. In the nightmarish scene more than 1,800 lives were extinguished one by one. A few were found alive in the water apparently trying to swim back to Japan and the Marines tried to save as many as they could. The desperation was not easy to witness and perhaps even harder to comprehend. It left Jim full of anguish and a general disgust of the dark side of human nature. No matter the race or the reason, people are people and pain is pain and death is simply ugly and cruel.

Saipan was conquered and the battle ended on July 24, 1944. Occupation duties were turned over to the Army's 27th Division and the Marines loaded their gear and departed. This time the trip was short, just five miles to the island of Tinian. Tinian is most famous as the launch point for the atomic bombs. The plane that carried out the mission, the *Enola Gay*, flew from Tinian. A smaller island than Saipan and covered mostly by sugar cane fields, the Americans transformed Tinian into one of the busiest airfields of the war.

One of the best examples of wartime strategy was played out during the Marines landing on Tinian. The Japanese were prepared for the Marines landing and they lay in wait on the beaches of Tinian Town. The 2nd Marine Division arrived and positioned off shore, but did nothing right away. No opening of doors and no release of men in landing vehicles. Meanwhile, the 4th Marine Division had landed, unopposed, on the other side of the island. Half the 4th Division made it ashore before the Japanese discovered the hoax. The plan undoubtedly saved American lives and Lieutenant Colonel Nelson K. Brown, Jim's commanding officer the Beach Master of the landing, later received a citation.

The fight for Tinian was similar to Saipan and Jim had pretty much perfected the role of gopher. Sealing caves; hauling water, ammo and equipment; retrieving bodies had all become a macabre routine. Tinian was also similar in the manner in which the Japanese Army and the island's natives retreat ended in suicide after suicide at steep cliffs overlooking the ocean. It was worse than a nightmare because there was never a merciful awakening, never the realization that it had all been just a horrible, vicious dream. The nightmare for many of World War II's surviving Marines has never really ended. The nightmare continued beyond the battle and followed them home and remained with them for the rest of their lives.

Victory on Tinian was achieved on August 1 and the men of the 4th Marine Division, including the wounded, boarded a merchant marine ship and headed in the direction of home. The conditions on the transport vessel were dire. Potable water was so scarce that if you could walk it was assumed you were healthy enough to go without water and make it through the duration with coffee. The problem was, Jim didn't drink coffee and he was beginning to think it was going to be a long ride home.

He was sure of it when he was assigned guard duty the first night. Jim patrolled a long corridor. All of the hatches that opened to the outside were covered with pairs of thick curtains. To come inside, a person would go through the first curtain and when it was completely closed they could go through the inner curtain to the inside of the ship. From a distance it looked as if they remained in complete darkness as they made their way out of enemy waters.

That night, one of the cooks who knew Jim didn't like coffee made him a cup with copious amounts of sugar and condensed milk, trying to disguise the coffee taste with the greatest of intentions. Unfortunately, the sea grew unusually violent and the heavy, sweet mixture churned in Jim's belly as the rough waves buffeted the ship. He was in pretty bad shape when his guard duty relief arrived and he was taken to sick bay where he was ironically allowed water.

Once they were back on Maui, Jim returned to his former job as the company clerk and replacements were added to the unit. The new men were full of questions and wanted to gather as much information as they could about the veteran Marines experiences. Some vets cruelly embellished their already horrific tales to scare the newbies. Some had collected gruesome "trophies" such as skulls and teeth. Jim thought this behavior was ridiculous and was not surprised when one of the replacements, too scared to face combat as it had been described to him, committed suicide.

Back in January, during his first stay at Camp Elliot, Jim had applied for Officer Candidate School (OCS). He had successfully passed all of the phases until he reached the last one which required an interview with the Marine Gunner who wouldn't give Jim his final signature because he felt a Marine needed combat experience to gain entrance to OCS. After the campaigns in Saipan, the Marshall Islands and Tinian, the Corps needed more officers. They noticed Jim had previously applied to OCS and asked him if he was still interested. Jim asked if he could have some time to think it over and rushed back to his tent to tell the guys about the offer. They were quick to remind him that OCS required a six year commitment to stay in the Corps. No further consideration was necessary and Jim turned right around, went back to command and told them his answer was a firm "no." He admits that they didn't take it too hard because they really didn't want to lose their only typist anyway so once again his typing skills may have saved him. Jim confessed that there were certainly moments later in the war when he thought back on his decision about OCS and cursed himself for turning down the opportunity.

Jim and the other men continued training and waiting for word of the next mission, not knowing when it would come or what it would be. Some of the Marines decided they might as well enjoy the surroundings while they waited and spent their liberty enjoying Haleakalä, the largest, extinct, open-mouth volcano in the world. The giant crater was filled with black volcanic sand. They would scramble down the steep sides, sometimes rolling to the bottom and then begin the exhausting effort to struggle their way back up amid the sinking sand just to do it again. Jim would think back to this experience later as some prescient preparation for what was to come; the infamous sands of Iwo Jima.

The word finally came and an enormous convoy consisting of the 3rd, 4th, and 5th Marine Divisions sailed out of Pearl Harbor. They really had no idea where they were headed. Some thought it must be time for the inevitable attack of mainland Japan. There was also a new rumor about an island called Iwo Jima, but to Jim it was just another Pacific island like all the others.

Jim had never considered himself overly religious, but religion had always been a part of his life. Every week growing up he had attended church with his family and Sunday school with his brother. He continued the practice of attending church while in the Marine Corps. Services were held on Sunday no matter where the troops were. There was always a few moments for worship no matter the circumstances. Jim went to services on Maui, while on transport ships, and even during the Roi-Namur, Saipan and Tinian missions. As he attended services during these battles he started noticing that the men he expected to see on Sunday were not there the next week. The absences became more clearly noticeable to him during these moments of quiet reflection and the loss of so many started to weigh on him. Rather than feeling a sense of solace, it just felt wrong. It was too painful mentally and he decided he just couldn't put himself through it again.

It was on the ship to Iwo Jima that he acceptably "gave up." Jim embraced a reckless, careless attitude that intensified wildly within him. On February 16, three days before arriving at Iwo Jima, Jim received a "Dear John" letter from his steady girlfriend and high school sweetheart, whom he had continued to write and receive love letters from throughout the war. He had considered their pledge to one another to be sacred and a foundation from which he drew strength.

The news affected him in a way that went beyond disappointment. It was as if everything hit him all at once; the stress of three intense combat missions; all the death and loss; the girl he thought he could always count on betraying him and the painful hole that was once filled by faith. It shook him to his core.

His seventy pounds of gear no longer felt heavy in comparison to the new burden he carried. A chip had been made in his psyche that day and over the years developed into a small crack that slowly continued to extend like tiny claw-like fingers reaching into his mind, heart and soul.

With so much hanging on his conscience when he hit the beach at Iwo Jima, Jim looks back sixty-five years later with a sense of overwhelming guilt, afraid that his "I just don't give a damn anymore" outlook may have caused harm to his fellow Marines. Jim's battle didn't end on V-J Day (Victory over Japan Day also known as Victory in the Pacific Day) and what started as a tiny fissure grew and spread with time.

For over six decades Jim waged a battle with himself. He never attended church again, his faith was gone. He would go on to raise two children of his own without religion and sadly watch them lead solitary, faithless lives and blamed himself. The growing, festering, malignant crack Jim faced is now understood to be Post Traumatic Stress Disorder (PTSD).

On February 19 the ship reached Iwo Jima, Jim stifled all the anxiety deep inside to concentrate on the mission. Once more he accompanied his commanding officer along with his body guard ashore. The CO was once again the Beach Master after his exemplary performance taking Tinian Island. They arrived at night while the rest of Jim's unit hit the beach the next afternoon. Jim reported to the first officer he came across and was again placed on "body detail."

Jim could tell at once that Iwo was going to be different than the other island battles. Iwo Jima was a mess. There was constant bombardment and the front lines were in chaos. The Japanese were entrenched in fortified tunnels and caves everywhere on the island. Jim immediately assumed his gopher duties, hauling water, ammo, and flame throwing equipment. There was not enough water and there were bodies everywhere.

Jim was moved from duty to duty and location to location and just tried to keep focus in all of the pandemonium. He took reassurance in the knowledge every Marine was concentrating on the mission and their task within the mission. Every Marine followed their orders and protected their fellow Marines. The Marine Corps remained a cohesive unit in the mayhem and that guaranteed success. They would not accept anything less. Failure was not an option. It had to be done so they carried on.

Two weeks into the battle Jim had night guard duty protecting a small compound they had established. The Japanese persistently infiltrated the American lines and were getting even better at it. The Marines had unfortunately established a habit early on of sending up flares at the same time each night and the Japanese quickly caught on. As a result, flares were now sent up pretty much continuously illuminating the sky steadily for the entire battle.

That night, as Jim peered into the dusty, smoky dimness he spotted five or six Japanese infiltrators. He reacted quickly, ducked through the perimeter wire and out after them. He knew he couldn't allow them to gain access to the American's stockpile of munitions and when he was close enough he engaged them in a fire fight. Jim was hit, but still managed to empty his magazine. Jim's foxhole buddy, Art Godfrey, had followed him out, saw he was hit and called for a corpsman. In shock, Jim stumbled and assumed he had just caught his foot on a rock, but when he looked down he saw that a shell had penetrated through his foot, boot and all. As he inspected his foot another shell bounced off his helmet with a loud 'ping' leaving a measurable dent as a memento.

Jim hobbled down to the beach and was unprepared for the gruesome carnage that met his weary eyes. There were dozens of fallen men covered with ponchos and many more waiting for treatment, barely clinging to life. With so many wounded men in need of help, the field hospital was in triage mode. Jim overheard conversations that no man would want to hear regarding which Marines had a chance at life and which Marines were so badly injured that their slim chances of survival made them a poor choice for the scarce resources of medical talent and supplies. The Marines with no hope were injected with morphine while the frantic caregivers concentrated their efforts on those who might survive. It was heartbreaking torture to witness.

The night Jim spent in the field hospital seemed to last forever. When dawn finally, mercifully arrived breaking through the gloom of the exhaustive night the wounded were moved to two hospital ships; the Samaritan and the Solace. Unfortunately, due to poor planning for this mission there were only two ships allotted which were just as inadequate as the field hospital had been to deal with the monumental carnage that was occurring on the island.

Jim, in better shape than most, was sent to a troop ship instead, the U.S.S Bolivar. The vessel had no medical facilities and so his wound received no medical attention. A total of 506 casualties were loaded on the troop ship, seven died before they left the harbor and were taken back ashore to be buried. Sixteen more men died on the way to Saipan and were buried at sea. The only thing Jim would say about the burials at sea was that they were unnerving to watch.

On the second day of the journey to Saipan, an American B29 bomber crashed landed on the ocean about 1,000 yards away from the Bolivar. There were four other ships in the convoy. The closest ship, the destroyer U.S.S Hudson, broke away and attempted to rescue the crew. The destroyer's crew was able to rescue eight of the twelve member crew. Six survived. The other four were determined to be lost at sea and after concluding the search efforts, the Hudson sank the remains of the bomber to eliminate any possibility of the Japanese gaining intelligence from it.

After reaching a hospital in Saipan, the bones in Jim's foot were put back together and his leg was wrapped in a cast. A week into his recovery he was roused from sleep and told to dress quickly. He was rushed to a Jeep which took him down to the boat dock where casualties were being loaded on a PBY seaplane. Large baskets hung from the plane's bulk-head, all but one filled with men in the full-body casts used to immobilize spinal injuries. Jim was to fill the final basket. The plane travelled only at night, again with no lights, utilizing the relative safety of the darkness and soon arrived at Johnson Island. From there Jim boarded another troop ship and ultimately ended up in Ford Island Hospital. It was at the hospital that Jim learned of President Roosevelt's death.

Jim was placed in a physical therapy ward with about twenty other convalescent Marines. He vividly remembered the screams from the bed next to his when a Marine awoke to discover his leg had been amputated. Surveying his roommates, Jim decided he was in relatively good shape and asked to be sent back to his unit on Maui. His doctors disagreed. Once again, Jim found himself on another troop ship, but this time it was headed to San Francisco.

In San Francisco the Marines were given new uniforms, some spending money and allowed a little well-earned liberty. After ten days Jim was required to fill out a form selecting the hospital he wanted to be transferred to. The form allowed for three requested locations, in priority order. Jim wrote Great Lakes Naval Hospital, Illinois in each of the three blanks, determined to complete his recovery close to home.

Typical of the Marine Corps they acknowledged Jim's request by sending him to Farragut, Idaho. Again, what initially seemed like a disappointment worked out in Jim's favor as he described Farragut as an absolute paradise. He was granted thirty days leave and flew back to Chicago on an Army transport plane and from there took a train to his hometown of Peoria. Luckily he arrived in time to visit his little brother who was home for a short time after just graduating from naval boot camp at Great Lakes, Illinois. The Blane family was together again after twenty months apart. It turned out to be a very nice visit home.

On the plane ride back to Idaho, V-J Day and the surrender of Japan was announced. The pilots landed the plane at the first available airport which happened to be in Denver, Colorado. Everything was crazy as everyone started to party in the streets. Jim obviously didn't know anyone in Denver but that didn't matter, he was one of the few men around in a Marine Corps uniform. He smiled confidently and claimed he is pretty sure he kissed every girl in town. When the hoopla dwindled down, Jim found himself back in Idaho working kitchen duty at the hospital. He delivered meal trays and fed the injured soldiers.

After a short time, Jim was transferred to a rehabilitation center in Oregon to be cleared for official discharge from the Corps.

While in Oregon one lazy Sunday afternoon, Jim decided while everyone was at church services to seize the opportunity and sneak into the first sergeant's office to use the typewriter to send a letter to his parents that they could actually read. To Jim's surprise the first sergeant didn't go to services that day either and caught him in the act.

Rather than being mad, the first sergeant was suspiciously happy and immediately called the commander to tell him that he had just found the unit a typist. In this situation it seemed that Jim's typing skills had actually worked against him, but only time would tell. His discharge was held in a frozen status and he was back to office work again, where it had all originally started in what seemed like a lifetime ago.

Jim did learn one very important lesson during his extended office stay in Oregon. The final step in the discharge process included an interview with the old master gunnery sergeant. It was his job to review the checklist and confirm everything was finalized and ready to go. As his last order of business he would ask every Marine the same question, "Do you wish to remain in the reserves?"

Every young Marine was fearful of the old, salty master guns and would reply respectfully, "Yes" whether they wanted to or not.

One day, Jim overheard an interview in which an older Marine responded to the final question with, "I have a choice, don't I?"

Jim was taken aback and from the sound of things so was the master gunnery sergeant, who replied, "Well….yes."

The Marine quickly responded with a defiant "No!" The Master Guns checked the "no" box on the form and the Marine's discharge was summarily completed without another word.

When Jim's discharge day did finally come, he also answered "No" to becoming a reservist and in doing so was ultimately saved from being called to duty during the Korean War.

Finally a "free man," Jim was considering staying in Idaho to attend college, but his mother wanted her first born home so badly that Jim hitch-hiked all the way from Idaho to Illinois and immediately enrolled in school.

Unfortunately, returning to life back home wasn't such an easy thing to do. Almost immediately Jim started showing symptoms of PTSD. He needed to numb the intense feelings that were starting to surface. He met up with some old high school friends, who were already heavy drinkers, and joined in as a means to drown the images, flash-backs and night terrors. At first it seemed like the best way to function as he attempted to assume the normal life he lived before the war, but he just couldn't adjust. He was doing the bare minimum in school to appease his mother as most of his time was spent cutting classes and drinking with friends. Jim was living with his parents and it was clear to them that something was wrong even before Jim wrecked the family car. They were at a loss and didn't know what to do.

In the 1940s there was no knowledge of how to address PTSD. Society's expectation was that the returning soldiers would just put their war experiences behind them and move on as if nothing had happened. One day they were on the battlefield watching their friends die and fighting for their lives and the next they were dropped back into their old lives with no way to process their feelings and experiences.

Life seemed to be moving at a whirlwind pace to Jim and he just pushed all of the pain and guilt of the war deeper inside himself. Jim continued his downward spiral until his high school friend and drinking buddy was found dead in a Chicago gutter. It was the shock Jim needed to see that he would suffer the same fate if he didn't make some changes. Jim wasn't sure exactly how to do it but he made a very conscious, deliberate decision to straighten his life out.

It has been said that the people we need come into our lives when we are ready. In Jim's case he was ready to meet the person he needed.

Jim didn't have, or even think he really wanted, a girlfriend after the "Dear John" letter he had received from his fiancée just before hitting the beach at Iwo Jima. A friend of Jim's wanted to bring his girlfriend home to meet his parents, but she wouldn't go without her chaperone, Nancy, and Nancy needed a date. Jim very unenthusiastically agreed to the blind date.

As it turned out, it was likely the best decision he ever made and Jim and Nancy married in 1953. Shortly after their marriage, Jim began work as a salesman for an insurance company, while Nancy, who worked as a flight attendant for American Airlines, was forced to quit her job because only unmarried women could work in the industry at the time. She was quickly able to land a job with Marshall Fields, a prominent Chicago department store.

Nancy's father was a construction engineer for Texaco Oil Company and invited Jim and Nancy to a company cocktail party. While at the party, Jim met a man who knew of a job at a very promising company and offered to make an appointment for him. Jim took him up on the offer, but was caught in a storm on the way to the interview. Jim remembered sitting in his car, trying to decide if he should pass on the interview or run through the rain and get his new suit wet. He knew he couldn't disappoint his in-laws so he braved the downpour, went to the interview and was offered the job. Jim worked at the Franklin Supply Company for the next thirty-four years.

The job with Franklin required the Blanes to move frequently. Jim and Nancy welcomed a baby girl while living in Atlanta, Georgia, in 1955 and a son two years later while living in New York City. Jim was eventually transferred to the company headquarters in Denver, Colorado, in 1959. He loved the area and moved from sales into management, eventually managing the branches in the five surrounding states that made up the Rocky Mountain region.

In the 1960s and 1970s the demand in the U.S. was growing for steel and pipe and domestic suppliers couldn't keep up. Franklin Supply

Company was forced to look for other suppliers so Jim began travelling overseas. He went to Germany, France and even back to Japan and handled many business deals in Tokyo. Jim held no ill will or animosity at all for the Japanese; in fact, he grew to love the beautiful country and its people. He understood that the Japanese soldiers in World War II were just doing their jobs by fighting for their cause and what they believed in, just like the Americans. Jim retired from Franklin in 1985 as a Senior Vice President.

Retirement hasn't really slowed Jim down much. He vows to welcome every challenge that comes his way, as he has throughout his life. After his retirement, he remained active on a number of boards and was the President of the Denver Petroleum Club. Jim is very proud of his children who have remained in the area. His daughter is a nurse and lives in Colorado Springs, while his son is a financial manager and works in Boulder. He is proud that they are both independent professionals that are financially secure. He is also proud that he could be an example of the power of a good education.

After forty years of skiing in the Rocky Mountains, Jim finally gave the sport up. Even though he has reached his eighties, he still manages to stay physically active by teaching pool and playing golf, a sport he took up at the age of five in 1929. Jim's true passion, however, is working with veterans and he finds peace and meaning in assisting other vets. He is involved in an assortment of veteran's organizations and helps wherever there is a need.

He is especially sought after as he can help veterans understand all of their government benefits and the copious amounts of paperwork that are required. Jim is known for carrying around his briefcase and producing the appropriate VA documents at the mention. Jim is thankful to be happy and healthy at the age of eighty-five AND still married to the wonderful Nancy. He is also thankful for his many good friends and the time to relax and enjoy them.

If you ask Jim about his personal definition of courage, he will say it is the willingness to take on a problem you don't believe you can solve, and keep chipping away at it until the mission is accomplished. Based on that definition, Jim considers the twenty-seven patriots, who were awarded the Medal of Honor on Iwo Jima, to exemplify courage at its finest and they are his heroes. He is quick to point out that it was unprecedented in military history to award twenty-seven Medals of Honor in thirty-six days on a seven and a half square mile island especially when you consider a total of eighty-two were presented to Marines for the entirety of World War II. The 6,852 that didn't come home, as well as those lost on other islands in the campaign, are also held in his high regard.

One specific World War II soldier, Paul Tibbits, earned Jim's respect. He was the pilot of the *Enola Gay*, the plane that dropped the atomic bomb, bringing about the surrender of Japan and the end of the war. Jim was impressed with Tibbits' display of class and composure while handling the criticism of his duty in the years following the war. The *Enola Gay*, named after Tibbits' Mother, flew from Tinian Island on August 6, 1945 and released "Little Boy," the code name for the bomb, over the Japanese city of Hiroshima.

Tibbits passed away on November 1, 2007, while in hospice care. He requested no funeral or grave marker to prevent anti-nuclear activists from creating a pilgrimage site. Instead his ashes were scattered in the English Channel per his wishes. Jim understood that Tibbits was just doing his duty in the war, like every other soldier and that Tibbits maintained the finest demeanor of a true soldier throughout the remainder of his life.

The most influential event in Jim's life was meeting Nancy. He believes she came into his life at the right time and helped him find the right path. He jokes that if he told Nancy everything he had been through during the war, she would surely have run the other way, however, in knowing them both personally, I find that extremely difficult to believe.

Jim is literally the "last man standing." All the other men from his unit have passed on. He was in contact with the last three, but recently he found himself alone. He is the last one to speak for them. Jim hopes that future generations can learn something from what he, and the men he fought beside, went through. The young people of today are the leaders of tomorrow and they will face similar issues and decisions about conflict and war. The best lessons are taught through personal experience by the people who lived it and can explain it firsthand. As the final voice, Jim hopes that someone somewhere is listening.

Jim's tireless dedication to veteran's causes is inspiring. It matters and it changes lives every day. All that you are embodies the traits I admire most; patience, focus, guidance and leadership. I am thankful for your calm presence, subtle courage and the manner in which you earned, not commanded, my respect. Jim is water; calm, smooth, flowing and deep.

Young Jim

Jim's mom

Jim, Dad, and brother
(1931)

A young Jim

FOR WINNER OF SOAP BOX DERBY

Winner of the Soap Box Derby tomorrow afternoon will be awarded a bicycle like the above in addition to getting a free trip o Dayton, Ohio, to compete for a college scholarship in the All-American Soap Box Derby there August 18 and 19. Prizes total- g $100 will be awarded other winners in the Soap Box Derby ere tomorrow.

Young Jim on horseback

Jim, playing basketball

Jim, in a casual moment

Jim posing in front of tent at Camp Maui.
The government censored his mail by crossing out
the camp name on the tent in the photo

Jim at work

Jim in Lahaina, Hawaii during the war

Jim standing at the same place 26 years later

Once Again, The Unimaginable

In March of 2010 these men returned to that fateful island. It was sixty-five years later almost to the day that they stepped foot back onto that black ashen sand. Now in their eighties it is the closure they need for a timeless peace.

They remark how it is not the island they remember. Time has changed it just as time has changed them. The island has become over grown with green grass and fresh vegetation just as love and peace has overgrown in the hearts of the men standing back on the very beach that tried to strip it all away. The change eases their memories. It softens the pain.

It is somehow easier to be here and know that time is not frozen back in 1945. Everything has moved on to a better place including here where hell on earth had once existed. It is so serene on Iwo Jima now, dare they think almost beautiful. The sky is clear and bright blue. The warmth of the sun shines down upon them as if it too is thanking them for the sacrifices they made here. The waves lapping the beach are tranquil and soothing, the complete opposite of the angry ocean that carried them here and shoved them ashore stealing their youth. However, their friends and also a part of themselves will remain lost here forever.

After a ceremony, prayers and the solemn moments spent reflecting here; these Marines once again do the unimaginable. They head up to the top of Mount Suribachi and set down, of all things, a golf tee. Max Brown sets his mind and his stance. Then with everything he has, for everything he has lost, with all the pain, sorrow, grief and anger experienced; in one fluid motion he dispels it all as he swings that golf club and sends that damn golf ball soaring into the ocean below. All the men take a turn and with a bold determination use that single shot to send it all deep, deep down into the bottomless, dark, blue sea.

They hurl it all away.

The Memorial at the top of Mt. Suribachi commemorating
where the flag raising took place. (Iwo Jima, 2010)

Don on the beach at Iwo Jima (2010)

Max teeing it off (Iwo Jima, 2010)

Afterword

There is no doubt that the thirty-six days on that island had a direct impact on Don, Max and Jim. This unique experience occurred at a peak moment in their development and nurtured them into the men they grew to become. Each of them handled the experience with grace. Each on their own terms, in their own ways Don turned to God, Jim turned away from God, Max surrounded himself with family and they all wanted to live life to the fullest.

These men and all the veterans of World War II carried the burden of the world and future generations when they entered that war and they carried the burden of compassion during the war. They lost friends and a part of themselves and placed all the horrors behind them to live normal lives. They didn't ask for the task.

And yes, troops want to come home, and families want them home, no one likes war. In fact, no one despises war more than those who have answered the call to fight it. I think that is a common misconception regarding the military. Yes, Marines have willingly agreed to sacrifice themselves for the greater good. But no one truly benefits from the horror, death and destruction and nobody knows that more than those witnessing it firsthand. Marines just want to do their job and do it well with the tools they need for success. Marines live and work by higher standards and accept nothing less from those around them. Don, Max and Jim willingly answered the call, got the job done and then came home and continued to lead dynamic lives inspiring everyone fortunate enough to be acquainted with them.

That makes them extraordinary men.

What impact on this world have you made? What influence on those around you, family and community have you had?

No one decides to be a hero. Improving a corner of the world doesn't take a hero. It just takes someone to put their own comforts aside, stand up and do the right thing for the right reason no matter how big or small.

Step out of your comfort zone and do something that makes a difference. If you are not afraid, then it is not a challenge. Face up to that issue that has lingered in the back of your mind, tackle it head on, hit the beach and take a stand. The proof you are growing is when you feel most uncomfortable. Don't be complacent with your life. So many fought, died, bled and suffered for your rights, to allow you to do what you want with your life. Do not let that effort be in vain. Do not waste the precious gift of life that God has given you or the gift of freedom that so many like Don, Max and Jim have secured for you.

THAT is what makes someone extraordinary.

When you boil it all down, in the end we are all people. We all have to abide by the laws established by our respective governments. All people have the same basic needs, wants and desires. But the raw human spirit yearns for freedom.

All people inherently want to be free.

Thank you, Veterans!

Post Traumatic Stress Disorder

There is truly no greater burden than the emotion of compassion during combat. The physical strength of carrying the seventy pound pack, weapon and gear does not compare to the load placed on the human spirit. The physical fatigue and emotional fatigue are nearly unbearable.

It takes a unique quality to live through the experience and not surrender empathy or kindness. These three men are testaments to that possibility. However, survival doesn't come without scars on the mind and soul that not only affect the sufferer, but those friends and family members around them.

Invisible wounds such as depression, survivor's guilt and Post Traumatic Stress Disorder (PTSD) after exposure to a distressing situation are common. Each has some similar symptoms and all are treatable. The stigma once associated with these issues as emotional weakness has long passed.

Because troops during war deal with life and death so intensely, they grow accustomed to living on the constant brink of ultimate awareness and fear. Since many are at such a young and developmental stage of human growth during their service they are discharged suffering with an affliction to some degree.

No one is immune and no one leaves unscathed. During World War I it was called "shell shock," and then it became labeled as "combat fatigue." But no matter what it is referred to as, the issues have always existed as long as there has been war. It was the Vietnam era that really brought these issues into the forefront and aid is more accessible than ever before.

Don Whipple explained it in an easy way to understand. He said combat veterans see and experience horrific atrocities, but don't have the time to deal with them or process them in the moment. These events are put away in a little box in the back of the mind and saved to worry about later.

Through the tour of duty and on throughout life, situations and circumstances that the individual could not cope with fill the box. Eventually the box becomes full and bubbles to the surface against a lid not equipped to handle the pressure.

The box begins to slowly leak; steam escapes and allows little instances to emerge resulting in symptoms like flashbacks, nightmares, suicidal thoughts and anger. Specific stimuli, for example a smell, can trigger an attack or episode. It is the body and mind's way of attempting to work out the issues, to open the lid on that box.

Sufferers may display signs of impairment, such as trouble sleeping and difficulty in relationships, not limited to family or spouses but also in occupations with supervisors and bosses. They may have issues in social settings and dealing with crowds or loud noises, an inability to express their feelings, because there are no existing words to articulate them.

It is imperative that with professional assistance the ugliness stored in that box receives the attention it deserves. Life is too short to stifle the pain inside when a full and productive life is available. It is never too late to empty that box once and for all. Please reach out for help. Healing is never overdue.

New research has yielded improved and effective treatments and I urge you if you are suffering, or you know a family member or friend struggling and living with any of these possible afflictions to please seek assistance immediately.

Resources

If you are in crisis, please call 911 or go to your nearest Emergency Room.

- United States Department of Veteran Affairs –
  National Center for PTSD
  WWW.ptsd.va.gov
  1-800-273-8255

- Military One Source
  WWW.militaryonesource.com
  1-800-342-9647

- SAMHSA - Substance Abuse and Mental Health Services
  Administration
  WWW.samhsa.gov
  1-800-622-4357

- Defense Centers of Excellence
  WWW.dcoe.health.mil
  1-866-966-1020

- Veteran Combat Call Center available 24/7
  To speak to a another combat veteran
  1-877-927-8387

- DStress
  www.dstressline.com
  1-877-476-7734

About the Author

Carron (Walpole) Barrella was born and raised on the south side of Chicago. Along with the structure and discipline of Catholic schools, having three brothers prepared her for life in the United States Marine Corps.

She earned the title of Marine at age 18 and served as a Military Policeman (5811). She met and married her husband while both were stationed in Iwakuni, Japan. They settled to make their home and raise their children outside Denver, Colorado.

Carron is an avid runner, tri-athlete and is a member of the Women Marines Association, as well as, Cooper's Troopers and other various veterans' organizations.

She also has a serious chocolate addiction!

Jim, Carron, Don, Max

CPSIA information can be obtained
at www.ICGtesting.com
Printed in the USA
FSOW04n0500190615
8017FS